An Action Research Proj
with SOLO Taxonomy

How to tell if it is
making a **difference**

Book 2

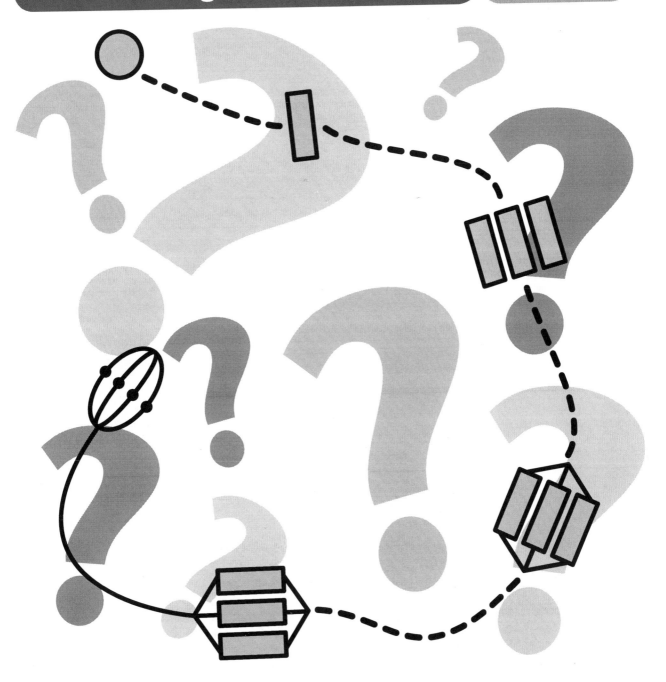

Pam Hook, Tabitha Leonard and Derrick Venning

essential resources

Title:	An Action Research Project with SOLO Taxonomy Book 2: How to tell if it is making a difference
Authors:	Pam Hook, Tabitha Leonard and Derrick Venning
Editor:	Tanya Tremewan
Designer:	Diane Williams
Book code:	5935
ISBN:	978-1-77655-222-1
Published:	2016
Publisher:	Essential Resources Educational Publishers Limited

United Kingdom:
Units 8–10 Parkside
Shortgate Lane
Laughton BN8 6DG
ph: 0845 3636 147
fax: 0845 3636 148

Australia:
PO Box 906
Strawberry Hills
NSW 2012
ph: 1800 005 068
fax: 1800 981 213

New Zealand:
PO Box 5036
Invercargill
ph: 0800 087 376
fax: 0800 937 825

Websites:
www.essentialresourcesuk.com
www.essentialresources.com.au
www.essentialresources.co.nz

About the authors:

Pam Hook is an educational consultant (HookED Educational Consultancy, www.pamhook.com), who works with New Zealand and Australian schools to develop curricula and pedagogies for learning to learn based on SOLO Taxonomy. She has published articles on thinking, learning, e-learning and gifted education, and has written curriculum material for government and business. As well as authoring and co-authoring more than 15 books on SOLO Taxonomy (some of which have been translated into Danish), she is co-author of two science textbooks widely used in New Zealand secondary schools. She is also a popular keynote speaker at conferences.

Tabitha Leonard (Neutrino Ltd, neutrino-ed.com) is the professional learning coordinator at St Kentigern College, Auckland, New Zealand, where she works with heads of department and many different teams to coordinate and lead the pedagogy of teaching and learning. She leads the whole staff during teacher only days, as well as focus groups such as the SOLO Taxonomy specialist teacher group and ICT lead teachers group. Her particular passion is e-learning, which she supports through professional development work and presentations at ULearn. Tabitha is currently completing her Postgraduate Diploma in Educational Leadership.

Derrick Venning lives in an ex-pit village in South Yorkshire, England where he finds constant motivation and inspiration for helping young people from disadvantaged backgrounds in building their futures. An experienced Head of Science, he specialises in turning around struggling departments. Derrick has also successfully led a range of whole-school initiatives, from those aimed at improving behaviour and outcomes of disadvantaged students to initiatives to prepare his school for the rigour of new government performance measures.

Contents

Introduction

It is a way of thinking: "My role, as a teacher is to evaluate the effect I have on my students." It is to know thy impact, it is to understand this impact, and it is to act on this knowing and understanding. This requires that teachers gather defensible and dependable evidence from many sources, and hold collaborative discussions with colleagues and students about this evidence, thus making the effect of their teaching, visible to themselves and to others. (Hattie 2012, p 19)

Teachers want to make a difference to student achievement. Given that almost everything teachers do will make a difference (Hattie 2009), a better approach is for teachers to focus on the extent of the difference they make. Through ongoing inquiry into their effect on student achievement outcomes, teachers can seek out and adopt approaches shown to have the greatest influence on student learning and achievement. They base decisions on research evidence about pedagogical practices that consistently enhance student learning.

For example, in Hattie's (2012, p 256) List of High Influences on Achievement, "developing high expectations for each student" has a massive impact on achievement (effect size of 1.44, markedly above the 0.4 hinge point or average effect). In contrast, the choice of open over traditional learning spaces ranks 145 out of the 150 influences (effect size of 0.01). For teachers wanting to maximise the difference they make, it is easy to see why a professional learning focus on modern learning environments might be of less interest than one on "developing high expectations" (Figure 1).

Figure 1: High and low influences on student achievement

High influence
High expectations for each student
ES 1.44
Rank 1

Low influence
Open versus traditional
learning spaces
ES 0.01
Rank 145

Note: Hinge point = 0.4; ES = Effect size; Rank out of 150 possible influences (after Hattie 2012)

The value of teaching as inquiry

When teachers embrace evidence-based teaching alongside teacher inquiry, to paraphrase Hattie (2012) they know their impact, understand their impact and act on their impact. They do this by observing their own practice and their students' outcomes using effective pedagogies such as the following, which are listed in *The New Zealand Curriculum* (Ministry of Education 2007, p 34):

- facilitating shared learning
- enhancing the relevance of new learning
- providing sufficient opportunities to learn
- encouraging reflective thought and action
- creating supportive learning environments
- making connections to prior learning and experience
- inquiring into the teaching–learning relationship.

Teaching as inquiry is increasingly seen as a necessary accompaniment to "evidence-based teaching".

John Hattie's ongoing Visible Learning meta-analytical research is enormously valuable in helping teachers identify effective pedagogies based on their relative influence on achievement. However, it does not negate the value of teacher inquiry – quite the reverse. Hattie (2012, p 12) is careful to identify that the "takeaway message" from the research is not that teachers should slavishly implement the interventions with the greatest effect sizes for raising achievement; rather they should carefully evaluate the effect of any intervention they use in their teaching practice: "know your effect".

Teachers evaluate the effect of what they do on student learning by asking, "What happened as a result of my teaching?" and "What are the implications for future teaching?" In doing so, they acknowledge that learning communities differ and what is highly effective in one setting with one group of students at one time may be less so in another setting, with another group or at another time. They must continually adapt and tweak learning interventions in response to changing student learning outcomes.

It can be difficult for classroom practitioners to "know their effect". They quite rightly worry about: what method they should use in teacher inquiry, what counts as an outcome, and the potential for bias. They ask if it is possible to know your effect without randomised controlled trials and meta-analyses. They do not want their pedagogical practice to rely on anecdote, opinion or ideology but they often lack the confidence and competence to undertake meaningful inquiry.

What this resource offers you

In our experience, schools using SOLO Taxonomy (Biggs and Collis 1982; Biggs and Tang 2007) as a model of learning often ask for advice on how to conduct teacher inquiry into the effect of their use of SOLO on student outcomes. This practical series, *An Action Research Project with SOLO Taxonomy*, is designed to answer these teachers and others who would like to conduct teacher inquiry in an achievable and effective way.

The first book in this series looks in depth at how to introduce and implement SOLO Taxonomy in the classroom and across the school. It includes a detailed case study of a comprehensive and thoughtful action research project on using SOLO in teaching and learning.

Some of the measurement issues raised in the first book are central to this second book. Here you will find details on the practitioner-based research methods schools can use to determine the effect of using SOLO with students so that schools can more easily contribute to the understanding and improvement of educational practice. The research methods cover both qualitative and quantitative approaches and all are user-friendly. Accompanying them are case studies from St Kentigern College (New Zealand) and Clifton Community School (United Kingdom).

This book is our contribution to helping teachers using SOLO-based approaches in their classrooms to "gather defensible and dependable evidence from many sources" so that they better "know thy impact" and, from there, can act on it.

1. Clarifying terms

The simple truth is that in education everything works somewhere and nothing works everywhere. (Wiliam 2015, p 28)

This section establishes the foundations for the discussion that follows by clarifying what we mean by:

- evidence-based teaching
- teaching as inquiry
- classroom-based use of SOLO Taxonomy.

What is evidence-based teaching?

Evidence-based teaching is teaching based on valid and reliable research into what works best to improve learning. It is an attempt to maximise achievement in schools by keeping a focus on interventions and teaching strategies that matter most – to change education into an evidence-based profession, much like what has already happened in medicine.

Asking teachers to use evidence-based pedagogies is not without challenge. Change is controversial. When shown studies that confront existing practices and ideologies, many respond in similar ways to the medical establishment when it reacted to calls for evidence-based medicine:

> The establishment considered evidence-based medicine an affront to their omniscience and authority, and dismissed it as both "old hat" ("everybody's already doing it") and a "dangerous innovation, perpetuated by the arrogant to serve cost-cutters and suppress clinical freedom." (David L Sackett: Interview in 2014 and 2015, **http://fhs.mcmaster.ca/ceb/docs/David_L_Sackett_Interview_in_2014_2015.pdf**, used with permission)

An important barrier to evidence-based teacher practice was substantially lowered with the publication of the meta-analytical work of Hattie (2009) and Marzano et al (2001). Hattie's initial work (published as Visible Learning) brought together "800 meta-analyses of 50,000 research articles, about 150,000 effect sizes, and about 240 million students" (Hattie 2009, p 1). These and subsequent meta-analyses are based on research comparing achievement outcomes across groups or over time. It is easily accessible research that has helped schools make sense of the different and often conflicting claims of single-study academic research where it was always possible to claim "research says" and find a paper to corroborate a particular position (Evans 2007).

It seems like common sense to respond to calls for evidence-based teaching by favouring practices with the highest effect sizes and rejecting those with the lowest effect sizes. However, Hattie (2012) cautions schools against simply selecting and implementing the interventions identified by their effect sizes as top strategies for raising achievement. He suggests a more powerful approach is to get the "gist" of strategies and approaches that best make teaching and learning "visible" to students and then to use teacher inquiry to identify their specific effects within your own context and conditions.

Hattie (2012) argues that by identifying the influences on these top strategies, what they rely on and what they have in common, we will be in a better position to:

- implement change in our classroom practice
- measure the consequences of any change we make to our teaching practice.

With evidence-based teaching, schools and teachers can take a more adaptive approach to teaching, moving away from a prescriptive, "one size fits all" practice. It opens the way for schools to conduct their own teacher or school inquiry into interventions likely to make the greatest difference in their community – interventions that:

> rely on the influence of peers, feedback, transparent learning intentions and success criteria, teaching multiple strategies or teaching using various strategies, and attending to both surface and deep knowing (Hattie 2012, p 84).

What is teaching as inquiry?

Teaching as inquiry goes hand in hand with evidence-based teaching.

To see teaching as inquiry, educators need to see the act of teaching as an ongoing inquiry into the impact of various (different and multiple) teaching methods on student learning. It involves asking which teaching method or combination of methods is best with these students in this context. Evidence-based teaching is deeply connected to teaching as inquiry because it provides rich data on a wide range of influential teaching methods and methodologies.

The steps in the process of teacher inquiry are deceptively simple. For example, the New Zealand Curriculum uses a series of question prompts (Figure 1.1) to encourage teachers to conduct skilled and active inquiry into the effect of the teaching strategies they use in the teaching learning relationship:

1. **Focusing inquiry:** What is important (and therefore worth spending time on), given where my students are at?
2. **Teaching inquiry:** What strategies (evidence-based) are most likely to help my students learn this?
3. **Teaching and learning using an identified strategy or combination of strategies**
4. **Learning inquiry:** What happened as a result of the teaching, and what are the implications for future teaching? Is there something I need to change? What are the next steps for learning?

As a result of Hattie's meta-analyses (Hattie 2009, 2012), interest is growing in "teachers as evaluators of the effect they have on student learning". In New Zealand, this has prompted a more rigorous approach to action research and the use of data (quantitative and qualitative) to show any change in outcome for students.

> Since any teaching strategy works differently in different contexts for different students, effective pedagogy requires that teachers inquire into the impact of their teaching on their students. (Ministry of Education 2007, p 35)

Figure 1.1: Teaching as inquiry

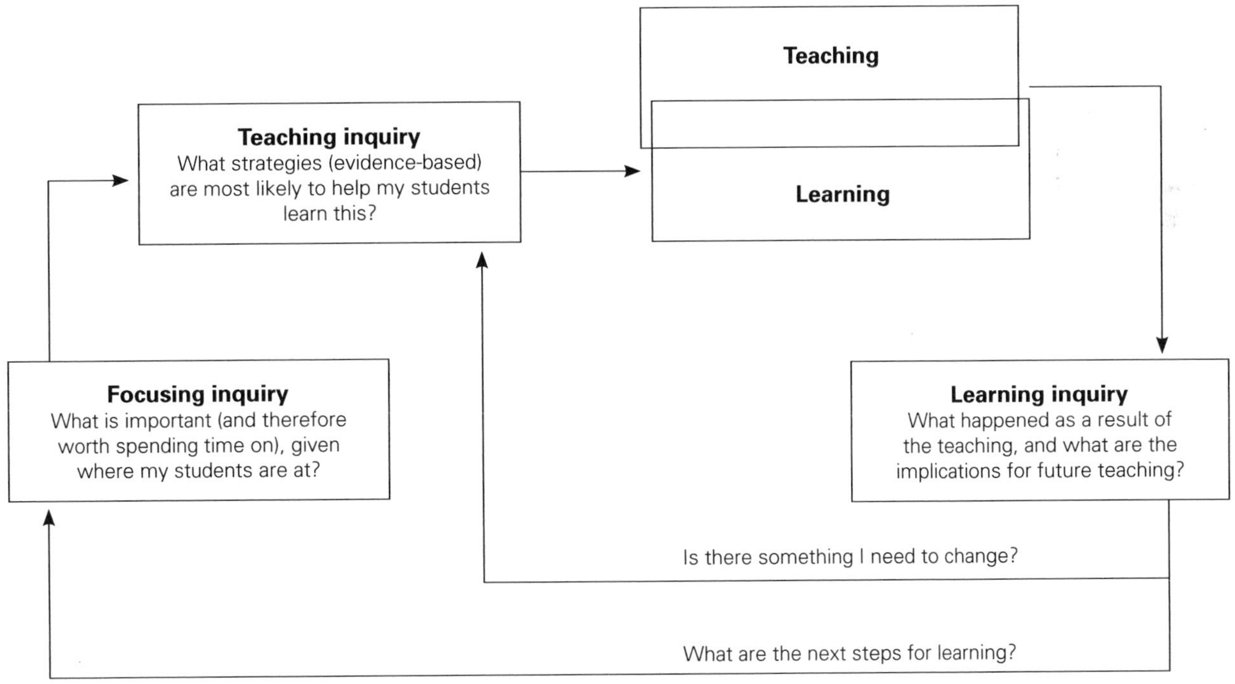

Source: Adapted from Ministry of Education (2007)

Problems and opportunities in teaching as inquiry

Evidence-based practice can lead us into difficulties when we ignore concerns about whether the "evidence" from either teacher inquiry or academic research is reliable and valid.

Using teacher inquiry to drive pedagogy. Designing research methodologies for teacher inquiry to determine what makes a difference is not easy. We recommend Braun and Clarke (2013), Cresswell (2012) and Flick (2014) as valuable professional reading for any teacher intent on creating research design for teacher inquiry that will not compromise the quality of the evidence used to inform practice.

Teacher inquiry has been criticised for its methodology, outcomes and potential for bias. For example, in a keynote address at the ResearchED Conference, Ben Goldacre (2013b) claimed:

> One of the most depressing experiences I've had is talking to teachers who describe a research project they have poured their heart and soul into that is methodologically crap.

Thus schools cannot simply assume that a teacher inquiry, however well-meaning, can be used to promote or defend a particular pedagogical approach. It is likely to fail on measures of reliability and/or validity for reasons such as the following:

- **Lacking critical review.** Teacher inquiries are seldom subject to academic review or published outside of the school community. Poor research design is not challenged, with the result that claims made are neither reliable nor valid.

- **Small sample sizes.** When the sample group studied is small, claims made for student outcomes may be reliable for the sample population but are not generalisable to others.

- **Correlation confused with causality.** Many teacher inquiries seek to identify the causes of their findings:

    > When I adopt teaching approach X, outcome Y happens to my students' learning.

    From this, they may then also assume that teaching event X is always followed by outcome Y. However, variable X may simply be a necessary but not sufficient condition for Y or merely increase its likelihood. Just because two events seem to vary in similar ways doesn't prove a relationship between them exists. If the methodological design of an inquiry is flawed, it is difficult to justify claims for causality and foolish for schools to use those findings as the basis for introducing wide-reaching pedagogical changes.

- **Unwarranted assumptions.** Teacher inquiries can make assumptions about the significance of the measure/data used as evidence. For example, they often present claims that "students loved it" or "they were highly engaged" as "evidence" to support a technology rollout or "flipping a classroom". However, even if students are "engaged" and "loved it", these findings are not reliable or valid indicators of their achievement or learning. Claims from studies like these cannot and should not be accepted in schools or by school communities as "evidence" for future practice.

- **Hawthorne and IKEA effects.** Study participants may put in more effort simply because they are taking part in research (a Hawthorne effect), and researchers tend to inflate the value of projects they have designed themselves (IKEA effect: Hattie and Yates 2014, p 306). Because of both these effects, claims that an intervention changes learning outcomes may be neither reliable nor valid.

    > [In the IKEA effect,] whenever someone takes an active role in the production of a positive outcome, then he or she is disposed towards valuing that outcome more positively, even to the point of overly inflated assessment, which the person believes is true, fair and correct. (Hattie and Yates 2013, p 306)

- **Misunderstanding the importance of "a shift" in student outcome.** With the release of Hattie's (2009, 2012) work on effect sizes, it is clear that in educational research it is the degree of shift in student outcomes – the "effect size" or the "magnitude of the change" – that counts. The concern is not simply with finding that those outcomes have shifted – such shifts need to be looked at with a more nuanced eye. As Hattie describes it:

    > Almost everything works. Ninety percent of all effect sizes in education are positive. When teachers claim they are having a positive effect on achievement or when a policy improves achievement this is almost a trivial claim; virtually everything works. One only needs a pulse and we can improve achievement. (Hattie 2009, p 16)

Using academic research to drive pedagogy. It is similarly problematic to uncritically rely on published academic research when the academic research cited is not based on randomised control trials, meta-analyses, effect sizes and other rigorous research practices. When the study is based on research that is not generalisable and/or when the number of third-party, direct replications of the research is limited, it is difficult to make any robust claims about next steps.

Examples of poorly designed research include early studies into educational programmes promoting the use of fear tactics to change student outcomes. Goldacre (2013a) describes how research into approaches that make sense and initially seem successful may on closer examination find results to the contrary. He illustrates his point with reference to the Scared Straight programme, in which children visited prisons to witness the consequences of criminal activity, with the idea that they would then be less likely to commit crimes in the future than children who had not been on the programme. But the problem for the researchers was that:

> the schools – and so the children – who went on the Scared Straight course were different to the children who didn't. When a randomised trial was finally done, where this error could be accounted for, we found out that the Scared Straight programme – rolled out at great expense, with great enthusiasm, good intentions, and huge optimism – was actively harmful, making children more likely to go to prison in later life.

More generally troubling is that a recent report of the publication history of the current top 100 education journals found that only 0.13 per cent of articles were replications (Makel and Plucker 2014). That is, it is extremely rare for academic research in education to have been verified by other researchers or even by the same research team.

And yet we need evidence from academic research and teacher inquiry in schools. Student populations in schools are diverse. Real opportunities for teacher inquiry arise because academic research into interventions and practices that show significant effect size shifts for one cohort of students may not be so effective with another. Schools wanting to know if what they are doing is making a significant difference for an identified group of students cannot simply rely on the findings from reputable academic studies or meta-analyses. They need to take the opportunity to conduct teacher inquiry into the effect of this intervention on student outcomes in their local context and to assess the reliability and validity of these claims over time.

> What does matter is teachers having a mind frame in which they see it as their role to evaluate their effect on learning. (Hattie 2012)

What is the classroom-based use of SOLO Taxonomy?

Sturcture of Observed Learning Outcomes (SOLO) Taxonomy is used in the classroom as a common language for teaching and learning between students and teachers.

The SOLO levels are used to differentiate surface, deep and conceptual levels of both learning task and learning outcome (Figure 1.2). The five levels of the taxonomy describe the different structures visible in student learning outcomes. Each level contains the level before plus a bit more:

 At the **prestructural** level there is no structure; the student response misses the point or simply repeats what is asked (*no idea*).

 The **unistructural** (*one idea*) and **multistructural** (*many ideas*) levels show a quantitative increase in what students know.

 The **relational** level restructures the components of the multistructural response by linking ideas to reach a deeper, more coherent understanding of the whole (*relate ideas*).

 The **extended** abstract level re-imagines the relational level response in new ways to reach another conceptual level and uses it as the basis for prediction, generalisation, reflection, or creation of new understanding (*extend linked ideas*).

The SOLO verbs aligned to each level are used as the academic language in the classroom. (Table 1.1 sets out a range of verbs classified by their SOLO level).

Figure 1.2: Annotated task sheet defining the levels of SOLO Taxonomy

My level of thinking and learning is ...	Learning task What is my level of understanding about SOLO Taxonomy?
Prestructural I am not sure about ...	The student has no prior knowledge of the key words in the question stem or is unsure and feels that they may misrepresent the question – that there may not be a connection between their understanding and the question title.
Unistructural I have *one relevant idea* about ...	The student may just be able to define or describe one aspect or element of the task question but is unable to explain its relevance or significance.
Multistructural I have *several ideas* about ...	The student may be able to define or describe at least three aspects which they feel relate to the task question but is unable to explain connections between these points or to the title.
Relational I have *several ideas* about ... I can *link* them to the big picture.	The student can explain/synthesise their ideas and confidently link these to the task question.
Extended abstract I have *several ideas* about ... I can *link* them to the big picture. I can look at these ideas in a new and different way.	The student can make connections beyond the material they are provided with by generalising, predicting and/or reflecting. This encourages the student to think synoptically, making connections drawn from real-world issues or concepts covered from other aspects of the topic or course. It prompts the student to think like a geographer, historian, scientist ...

Annotations:

Learning task can reflect the objective for the lesson.

This level is crucial, as it allows students to take risks and suggest an idea even if they are unsure. It also ensures that all students can participate and at least begin to engage with the task question.

Distinctive level names helps students to memorise and "unpack" meaning.

Three points are suggested here to make a clear distinction in the level of progress from unistructural.

Diagrams reinforce student understanding of the level of their learning.

Sentence starters support literacy and thinking about learning.

Table 1.1: SOLO declarative and functioning knowledge verbs

SOLO level		Verbs
Unistructural		define, identify, label
Multistructural		describe, list, outline
Relational		sequence, classify, explain, compare, contrast, analyse
Extended abstract		generalise, predict, evaluate

With a model that makes the structure of a learning outcome visible, students and teachers can explicitly describe the cognitive complexity of any learning task and the cognitive complexity of any learning outcome. As SOLO provides a common language of learning, students can see learning through the eyes of their teacher, and the teacher can see learning through the eyes of the student. Furthermore, because task and outcome can be at different levels (differentiated), SOLO can be used in classrooms as a nuanced language when:

- giving feedback
- describing prior knowledge
- planning differentiated learning intentions and success criteria
- thinking about thinking (metacognitive reflection)
- choosing strategies (thinking or e-learning) to complete tasks
- determining prior knowledge
- attending to both surface and deep knowing.

All of the above elements are associated with influences that make the greatest difference to achievement gains in Hattie's meta-analyses.

2. Teaching as inquiry with SOLO Taxonomy

SOLO gave us the tools. SOLO gave us a structure. SOLO provided for us transparently the maps, the tools, the rubrics, that we could now better understand what it was we were asking students to do. We were able to move from pretty superficial surface-type questioning or understandings, move into deeper and more complex understandings and the students knew what we were doing – it was not a magical mystery tour. (Roland Burrows, Principal (Secondary), St Andrews College 2013)

When schools adopt the classroom-based use of SOLO to make learning visible to students and their teachers, they should also conduct teacher inquiry into the effect of this practice. What difference does sharing SOLO as a model of learning make to student learning? What difference does it make when students use SOLO as their own model of learning?

This section takes you through some key questions to ask and answer as you set up your teacher inquiry:

- Why are you doing it? – identifying the goals, the desired outcome
- What is the question? – identifying the research questions that will measure this outcome, the success criteria
- What counts as an answer? – identifying how you will know if what you are doing has made a difference
- What do they already know and do? – measuring students' prior knowledge.

We end this section with two case studies that demonstrate some of the approaches teachers have taken to answering these questions.

Why are you doing it?

The first step is to identify the goals of your study. Why do you wish to use SOLO with students? What achievement outcome are you seeking to change?

Schools commonly adopt the classroom-based approach to SOLO to help make learning visible to teachers and students. Schools have identified that establishing a common language of learning using SOLO levels and academic verbs is important and worth spending time on given its benefits for learning. It is not uncommon for secondary schools with an assessment-driven culture to seek improved academic results (such as Merit and Excellence endorsements in New Zealand) for students as a consequence.

Making learning visible can be interpreted and achieved in different ways. For example, SOLO may be used to make learning visible in contexts such as the following:

- **Feedback** – students (and teachers) use SOLO as a way to provide effective feedback and feedforward.
- **Task** – teachers (and students) use SOLO to create explicit, proximal and hierarchical learning intentions and success criteria.
- **Metacognition** – students use SOLO as a means of measuring and identifying progress when determining:
  - the level of complexity of a learning task (where am I going?)
  - how well they are accomplishing the task (how am I going?)
  - the activities they need to do next (where to next?).
- **Process** – students (and teachers) use SOLO to select effective strategies to support the task. Students will be able to determine the strategies needed to undertake the task: What are the strategies needed for bringing in ideas, linking ideas and extending ideas? What thinking strategy will be useful for linking ideas?
- **Prior knowledge** – students (and teachers) use SOLO to measure prior knowledge: What is my level of understanding about the topic before we start?
- **Attending to both deep and surface knowing** – students (and teachers) use SOLO to access effective differentiation by planning for both surface and deep knowing (constructive alignment): What steps in learning will lead students from surface to deep understanding of the discipline or concept?
- **Self and peer assessment** – students use SOLO as a means of self and peer assessment.

What is the question?

The next step after deciding on why you want to share SOLO with students (desired outcome) is to formulate the research questions and check that the questions can be answered in the context of the resources available.

What counts as success when we make learning visible to students and teachers (success criteria)? How will we know if making learning visible is working? And to what extent does this increased visibility enhance student learning?

We can ask students about their experiences when using SOLO as a model of learning. For example:

- What has been your experience of using SOLO as a model of learning? (*description*)
- What factors, contexts or situations have influenced your use of SOLO? (*description*)
- Why did these factors, contexts or situations influence your use of SOLO? (*explanation*)
- To what extent did these factors, context or situations influence your use of SOLO? (*evaluation*)

The responses to these and other generic questions can be used to inform more specific teacher inquiry. For example:

- How do students use SOLO as a common language with their teachers?
- How do students use SOLO when they plan, monitor, control and regulate their learning?
- How do students use SOLO when they give and receive feedback?
- What are student perceptions of the impact of using SOLO to determine what they are doing, how well it is going and what they should do next? How do students' perceptions of their learning align with their teachers' perceptions?
- What factors influence a student's decision to make SOLO "my model for learning"? Why do these factors influence students? To what extent do these factors influence students?
- What factors influence a teacher's decision to embed SOLO in their teaching practice? Why do these factors influence teachers? To what extent do these factors influence teachers?
- How does using SOLO change the way students think about and monitor their learning?

What counts as an answer?

Next, think about the data you are collecting in response to the research question and how you will know from the data if what you are doing has made a difference. What measures will you use as evidence of the impact on student learning? What criteria will you use to measure the impact? What is the anticipated outcome? What will it look like? Will the measures be quantitative and/or qualitative?

Knowing what counts as an answer will help you to identify a suitable research method and sample size. The following are some examples of different approaches you might take:

- If you are evaluating the outcome of an educational practice, then it is likely you will undertake a comparative investigation in which you use data (text and/or numbers) to measure change over time or change between groups. For example, you might use the effect size of the intervention on the student sample between groups or over time; or compare groups in a randomised trial in which students are randomly assigned to one of two groups.
- If you are interested in "what students experienced" when using SOLO as a common language of learning and "how" they experienced or "see" SOLO as a model, then it is likely you will undertake a phenomenological investigation.
- If you are trying to find patterns or commonalities in use of SOLO by teachers or students, then a narrative study, case study or even an ethnography may be appropriate.

You need to think about the amount of time and the resources required in any decisions about what counts as an answer and about the research design. For example, if you are planning to conduct an online survey with students, then you need to think about practical factors such as the time needed to create the survey, organise time for the participants to complete the survey, follow up on non-participants, and collate and analyse the results.

Before choosing your final design, you may look at several options (case study, comparative study, retrospective study, snapshot, longitudinal study). Your choice of design should align with the intent of the research question and be appropriate for the target group of participants.

What do they already know and do?

You can use the desired outcome and the success criteria you have already established to then measure students' prior knowledge.

To avoid sorting out a problem that does not exist, it is important to establish that the students do lack an understanding of the learning you are targeting before launching an intervention. You therefore need to collect some kind of baseline audit on student knowledge, skills, attitudes and behaviours when learning. Identify the extent to which students are using a common language, their knowledge of surface and deep knowing and whether they struggle to choose relevant next steps for learning.

Useful SOLO strategies for determining students' existing levels of understanding are open-ended tasks, SOLO-differentiated questions, prompts or tasks, SOLO hexagons and even SOLO hand signs (Figure 2.1). Case study 2 below demonstrates the use of SOLO hexagons for this purpose. For more information on all of these strategies, see *First Steps with SOLO Taxonomy* (Hook 2015).

Figure 2.1: Using SOLO hexagons and SOLO hand signs to determine students' prior knowledge

(a) SOLO hexagons – students create tessellations to show connections among ideas

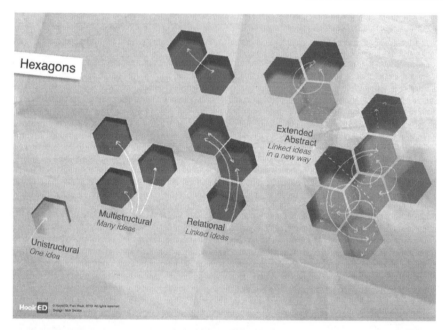

(b) SOLO hand signs – students signal their own SOLO level of understanding

By determining the prior knowledge of your students, you can gain a more nuanced insight into the cognitive complexity of their understanding before they experience the intervention you are researching. Does their initial understanding have the structure of many loose ideas (multistructural), making links between ideas (relational) or extending linked ideas in new way (extended abstract)?

The next step in teaching as inquiry is to teach using an identified classroom-based approach to SOLO, and then re-administer the outcome measure(s) to assess any change in achievement outcome. That change may be qualitative and/or quantitative and determined using measures of effect size or numerical data or through comparing themes or patterns in student and teacher discourse. For more information on approaches and strategies for determining change and the significance of any change, see Sections 3 and 4.

Note: Whatever method you use to determine change, always bear in mind that you need to be cautious in any claims you make about your findings. If your research shows an instructional method produces optimal learning outcomes, it is necessary to replicate these findings with other groups of students in other schools before you can claim the instructional method is more generally effective.

Approaches to answering teaching as inquiry questions

The following case studies demonstrate two approaches teacher researchers have taken to examining the impact of a SOLO intervention. The first involved an inquiry into the use of SOLO maps and rubrics, while the second focused on SOLO hexagons.

Case study 1: SOLO maps and rubrics

In this case study, the teacher researcher assessed changes in the complexity of students' understanding after students used SOLO maps and rubrics when learning a new concept.

The set-up

This case study involves a co-educational Year 12 chemistry class of mixed ability (NCEA Level 2E).

Structure and bonding in Year 12 chemistry is a completely new concept when it comes to justifying molecule shape. SOLO maps and a SOLO thinking model were prepared to walk students through all of the parts or factors that affect molecule shape, with the aim of working them up to an extended abstract level of understanding.

Levels of achievement for the learning outcomes below (listed under "The tasks") and the other learning outcomes were compared using the end-of-topic test and examination results. The results were used to answer the question: Does the use of SOLO maps increase students' understanding from a unistructural or multistructural level at best?

The tasks

In groups, students broke down the different components that determine a molecule shape and polarity. They added these components to customised SOLO maps for various molecule examples. The intended learning outcomes for this task were as follows:

1. Identify the shape of simple molecules using the VESPR (valence shell electron pair repulsion) model. (For this they used the HOT SOLO Compare and contrast map illustrated in Figure 2.2.)

2. Understand that covalent bonds can be polar or non-polar depending on the electronegativity difference between the atoms in the molecule and that there is a non-polar–polar–ionic continuum. (For this they used the HookED SOLO Describe++ map illustrated in Figure 2.3.)

3. Predict the polarity of molecules using bond polarity and shape (restricted to those having no more than four electron pairs about any atom, including multiple-bonded species). Describe bond polarity in terms of the electron-attracting power (electronegativity) of the bonded atoms.

Figure 2.2: HOT SOLO Compare and Contrast map used for Year 12 chemistry task

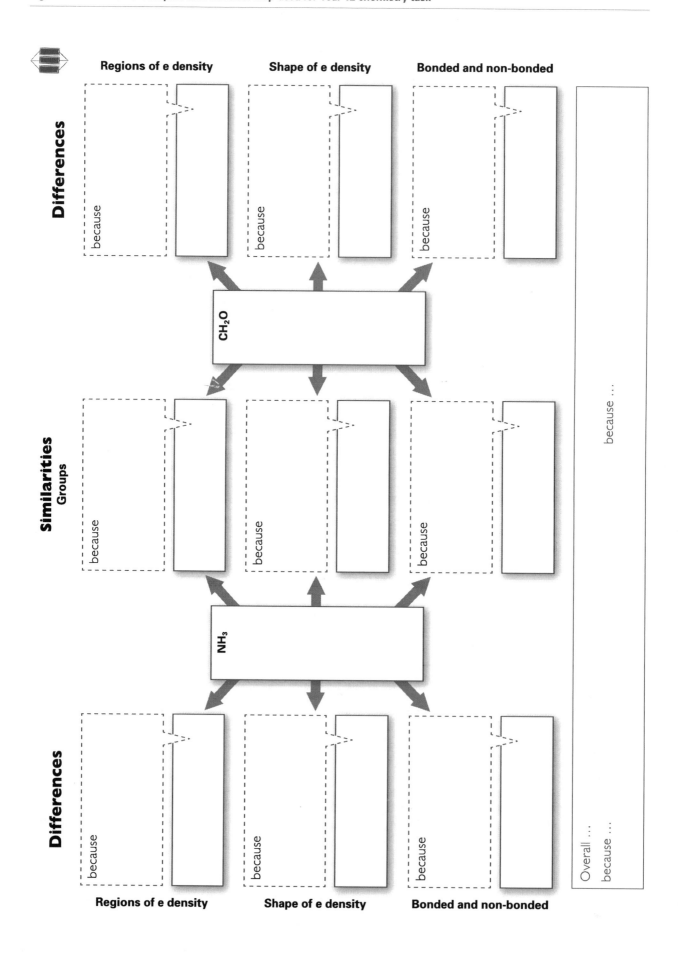

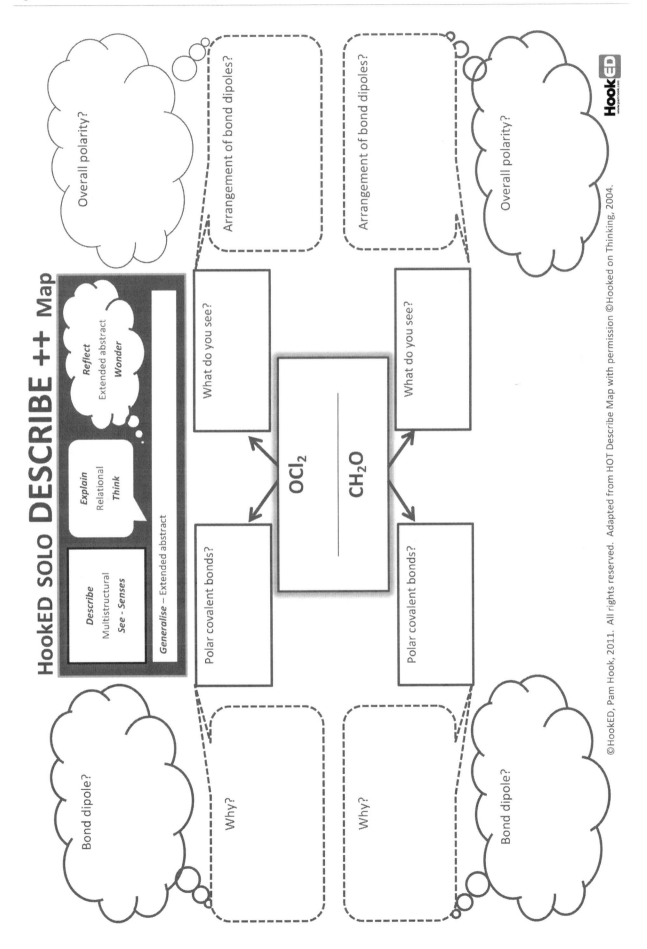

The inquiry outcomes

The outcomes were measured by analysing topic test answers and end-of-year examination answers and comparing them with students' answers to other questions in the same achievement standard (2.4) that were not taught using the SOLO thinking model.

Data collected showed that:

- the average mark for molecule shape and polarity question in topic test, taught using a SOLO thinking model, was E7 (lower Excellence)
- the average mark for other questions in the same standard, not taught using SOLO thinking model, was M5 (lower Merit, two grades below E7 on an eight-point scale).

In **interviews** at the end of the year, students reported that they found revising molecule shape and polarity was much easier than it was for the other concepts. They felt that they had a deeper understanding at the time of teaching so needed to do less revision on this topic.

Case study 2: SOLO hexagons

In this case study, the teacher researcher used SOLO hexagons to determine prior knowledge and as an intervention for learning to identify any shifts in understanding as a result of using SOLO hexagons to connect ideas.

The set-up

This case study involves a co-educational Year 12 chemistry class of mixed ability (NCEA Level 2). The SOLO hexagons activity was used before and after teaching the topic to formatively assess students' prior knowledge and their subsequent learning.

The tasks

1. Individually, students were given a set of hexagons that had key phrases and concepts for the new topic, reaction kinetics. Concepts within this topic are well covered in Level 1 science, so students came to the class with a reasonable level of prior knowledge.

   The students' task was to match up as many hexagons as possible and then record the result in a digital photograph.

   The hexagons were then placed in an envelope and kept aside until students had completed the series of learning outcomes for reaction kinetics.

2. At the end of the topic, students were given the set of hexagons again to match up as many of them as possible (as at the beginning of the topic).

3. Students then compared their old hexagon tessellation diagram with their new diagram, and justified to their neighbour the links they had made and any differences between the diagrams.

The inquiry outcomes

From **student interviews**, feedback included:

> By doing this, I was able to understand it, and talk about it a lot with my neighbour.

> I found this topic quite hard – it was a broad topic, and after working on this it helped me categorise my ideas and relate them.

Outcomes of using SOLO hexagons to determine prior knowledge at the beginning of the topic, or of a set of related learning outcomes, were that the teacher could group students according to depth of prior knowledge and differentiate learning tasks accordingly. These outcomes were achieved with two different approaches to the activity, where each student was given either:

1. a set of **blank hexagons** at the beginning of a topic on rates of chemical reactions, with the task of writing any key phrases that they knew about the rates of reaction and showing, if they could, how these phrases could be linked together, or

2. a set of **hexagons with key phrases** and concepts for the rates of chemical reactions, with the task of showing, if they could, how these phrases could be linked together.

Both of these tasks can be developed throughout a topic. Initially students made very few connections and had difficulty applying the concepts to specific examples. However, as the topic progressed, students were able to make more in-depth links and apply justifications to different situations.

> I really enjoyed using the hexagons as they helped me link ideas together, and I could see how my understanding grew throughout the topic. This gave me confidence to answer the more technical questions. (Year 12 student)

A note on SOLO hexagon resources

For detailed information on how to use SOLO hexagons, see *First Steps with SOLO Taxonomy* (Hook 2015).

Resources available to create SOLO hexagons include:

- the online HookED SOLO Hexagon Generator (**http://pamhook.com/solo-apps/hexagon-generator**), which you can use to add content to hexagons. Once this tool has generated the Word document, you can add images, photographs, colour, different fonts etc
- SOLO hexagon templates (**http://pamhook.com/wiki/SOLO_Hexagons**).

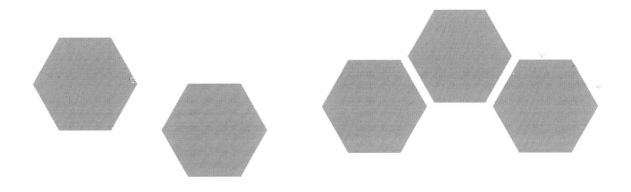

3. Using words as evidence – qualitative data

I find that using the [SOLO] rubrics with the classes, I am having deeper conversations with my students about their learning. (Teacher reflection, Mr Ross Gerritson, Head of Department of Music, St Kentigern College)

Qualitative data come from words. Qualitative data identify and interpret meanings in a local context rather than seeking the average response, comparing two groups based on number of responses or looking for cause and effect. This type of data is valuable for school and teacher inquiry because this research must take account of context and a diverse student body – and "any teaching strategy works differently in different contexts for different students" (Ministry of Education 2007, p 35).

Section 4 introduces the counterpart to this approach: quantitative data (numbers) and quantitative research, which relies on surface data from many participants to make statistically significant claims. For many teacher researchers, it may be difficult to undertake generalisable quantitative research with a small sample size of 15 to 30 students per class.

In contrast, with qualitative research teacher researchers collect detailed and rich data from fewer participants. Saturation sampling levels, where additional sampling does not uncover new information, can be met in qualitative studies with 15 to 30 participants. When teachers choose qualitative research, the student is also less defined as a member of a statistical population — a data profile – and more as a person, a member of a social domain or a learning community.

This section begins with a brief introduction to tools available for qualitative research. Its main focus is then on two methods of qualitative analysis suitable for use in teacher inquiry: thematic analysis and interpretative phenomenological analysis. Each of these methods is described along with relevant examples from teacher inquiry at St Kentigern College.

Tools for collecting and using qualitative data

Qualitative data can come in the form of written, oral and visual text. Teacher researchers may collect these data from observation, interviews, focus groups, and/or surveys of individuals or small groups.

With online audio distribution platforms like SoundCloud (**https://soundcloud.com**), teacher researchers can easily store and retrieve sound files. Many use mobile smartphones or live webcams to collect word data for later analysis.

Online text analytic tools help transcribe (eg, voice to text diction apps on mobile phones) and sort the word data collected. They allow faster analysis by speeding up word frequency counts that can help identify themes. Figure 3.2 demonstrates how online tools can be used for text analysis based on an excerpt from a video interview with Roland Burrows, Principal (Secondary) at St Andrew's College, Christchurch (Figure 3.1). The screen shots show results from:

- Voyant cirrus cloud, which analyses word frequency
- Voyant links, which finds collocates for words and displays links between them. It shows term frequencies in proximity to each keyword
- Voyant tools "reveal your text" overview (see **http://voyant-tools.org**).

Figure 3.1: Interview with Roland Burrows, "So why SOLO at St Andrew's College?"

For the interview, got to: **https://youtu.be/zuwcRFmHQBw**

Figure 3.2: Text analysis using Voyant tools

(a) Voyant cirrus cloud

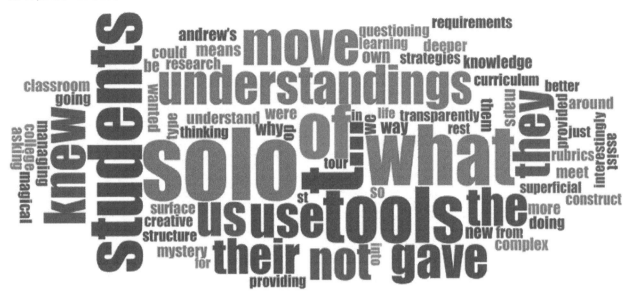

(b) Voyant links

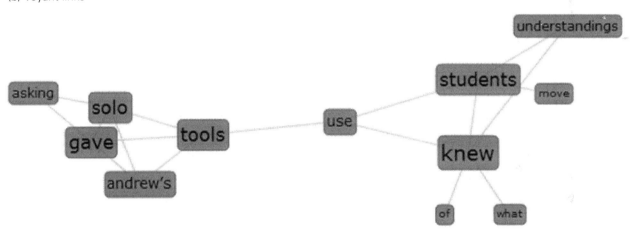

(c) Voyant tools "reveal your text" overview

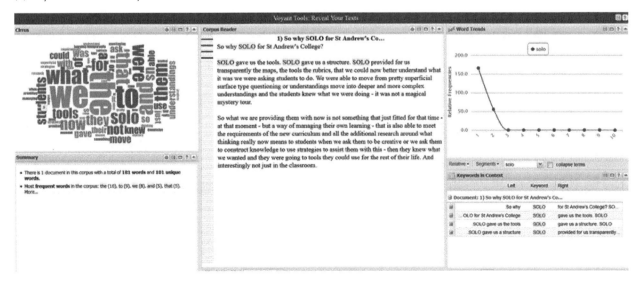

Thematic analysis

In thematic analysis, the teacher researcher looks for patterns and themes across a text-based data set of student or teacher responses (Figure 3.3).

Examples of sources of the data include a qualitative survey of responses to one or more open-ended questions, images and/or video, interviews, student diaries or learning logs, self and peer assessments, vignettes, story-completion tasks, and narrative story tasks. The participant sample may be from an individual student (or teacher) or from a sample of students using the classroom-based approach to SOLO.

The teacher researcher is looking for various themes as "told" by the participants from their perspective. The teacher researcher may identify the themes from the data and/or impose themes drawn from other sources. For example, if exploring reasons why students or teachers use SOLO, the teacher researcher might look for imposed themes such as:

- common language
- confidence in learning
- student agency
- knowing next steps
- importance of effort
- importance of strategies, differentiation, feedback and feedforward
- higher-order thinking
- deep and surface understanding
- direct instruction
- questioning
- metacognition.

Online research tools, such as TAPoR (www.tapor.ca), are helpful for this kind of textual analysis.

Below we look at a range of methods for collecting your data set and analysing it, before presenting a case study that illustrates the use of thematic analysis.

Figure 3.3: Process in thematic analysis

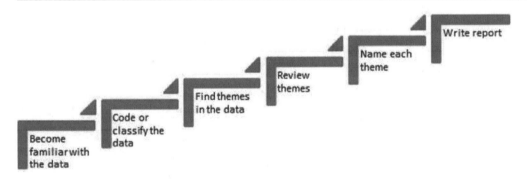

Data collection using open-ended questions

Open-ended questions and the structured interview are commonly used to assess student use of self-regulatory learning strategies (Zimmerman and Martinez Pons 1986). In this approach, teachers:

- select the question or questions most suitable for prompting an open-ended response
- collect responses from participants
- read and re-read the responses, looking for common themes in the data
- code the data using these themes
- analyse the findings and draw conclusions.

Table 3.1 lists some samples of open-ended questions to give a sense of a range of ways you might use to frame your own questions.

Table 3.1: Sample of open-ended questions

- What do you think about learning?
- Can you tell me *how you know you are learning*?

  Do you have one or more methods to help you learn and remember? What methods do you use? How often would you use each one?

- Can you tell me how you assess *what you know before you start*? (Measure prior knowledge)

  Do you have one or more methods to help you measure what you already know? What methods do you use? How often would you use each one?

- Can you tell me how you *plan your progress* when you are learning? (Differentiate tasks)

  Do you have one or more methods to help you bring in ideas? What methods do you use? How often would you use each one?

  Do you have one or more methods to help you link or make connections between ideas? What methods do you use? How often would you use each one?

  Do you have one or more methods to help you think in new ways about or extend ideas? What methods do you use? How often would you use each one?

- Can you tell me how you *measure your progress* when you are learning? (Differentiate outcomes)

  Do you have one or more methods to help you measure changes in your learning over time? What methods do you use? How often would you use each one?

- Can you tell me how you know *how well you are learning*? (Self-assessment)

  Do you have one or more methods to help you know how well you are learning? What methods do you use? How often would you use each one?

- Can you tell me how you know *how well others are learning*? (Peer assessment)

  Do you have one or more methods to help you know how well others are learning? What methods do you use? How often would you use each one?

- Can you tell me how you know *what to do next* in your learning? (Feedforward)

  Do you have one or more methods to help you know what to do next? What methods do you use? How often would you use each one?

- How do you feel *when you get stuck* in your learning? What do you do?

  Do you have one or more methods to help you when you get stuck? What methods do you use? How often would you use each one?

- Can you tell me how you *plan your writing*?

  Do you have one or more methods to help you when you plan your writing? What methods do you use? How often would you use each one?

- Can you tell me how you *motivate yourself* to learn?

  Do you have one or more methods to help motivate you to learn? What methods do you use? How often would you use each one?

Sample wrap-up questions (after Braun and Clarke 2013)

- Is there anything else you think we should know about the way you learn? (Self- and peer-assess learning; measure prior knowledge; give effective feedback and feedforward on your learning; measure how well you are progressing in your learning; choose effective strategies for learning; differentiate your next steps in learning etc)

- Are there any questions we should have asked about the way you learn but didn't?

Collecting student responses to images and next step suggestions to written learning outcomes is another effective way of collecting word data about the classroom-based use of SOLO Taxonomy. For example, you might conduct a "What does this text show?" exercise in which students are to identify examples of different SOLO levels in a written learning outcome and suggest next steps (Table 3.2).

Table 3.2: Student responses to written learning outcomes at three SOLO levels

Original task

Discuss why magnesium chloride has the formula $MgCl_2$ whereas sodium chloride has the formula NaCl.

In your answer, include:

- the charges of the ions that make up each compound
- the ratio of atoms
- the overall charge of each compound.

Student response to written learning outcomes: Underline the loose ideas (multistructural), highlight the linked ideas (relational) and circle the extended ideas (extended abstract).

(a) Extended abstract outcome (linked ideas extended)

Both $MgCl_2$ and NaCl are 'electrically neutral' ionic compounds so that the total +ve charges in each compound balances the total −ve charges.

Both $MgCl_2$ and NaCl contain chloride ions Cl^{-1} because chlorine atoms [2,8,7] react by gaining an electron to form chloride ions $[2,8,8]^{-1}$.

The metal ions in the two ionic compounds have different positive charges.

Magnesium ions have a +2 charge Mg^{2+} $[2,8,]^{2+}$ because magnesium atoms [2,8,2] become magnesium ions $[2,8]^{2+}$ when the atom reacts by losing two electrons.

Sodium ions have a +1 charge Na^{+1} because sodium atoms [2,8,1] become sodium ions $[2,8]^{+}$ when the atom reacts by losing one electron.

Overall the difference between formulae $MgCl_2$ and NaCl is because of the different charges on the metal ions:

- the charge on each magnesium ion (Mg^{2+}) is balanced by the charge on two chloride ions (Cl^-) – formula ratio 1:2
- the charge on each sodium ion (Na^+) is balanced by the charge on one chloride ion (Cl^-) – formula ratio 1:1.

(b) Relational outcome (linked ideas)

Mg stands for magnesium and Na stands for sodium and Cl stands for chloride.

At the start each ion is either positively or negatively charged.

Magnesium ion was Mg^{2+} which means it lost two electrons to become stable and positively charged. Two of the Cl^{-1} is needed as to balance out the Mg^{2+} as resulting in a neutral ionic compound.

Na^{+1} loses one electron to become stable and positively charged and Cl^{-1} gains one electron so they only need each other to form a neutral ionic compound.

One atom gains electrons to form a full valence shell while the other atom loses electrons to do the same thing.

continued ...

(c) Multistructural outcome (loose ideas)	

Magnesium and chlorine join together to form an ionic compound.

$Mg^{2+} + Cl^{-1} \rightarrow MgCl_2$

There is a two which represents number of ions. Electrons will either need to be gained or lost.

Whereas with sodium chloride the sodium and chloride just completely cancel each other out.

$Na^+ + Cl^{-1} \rightarrow NaCl$

To gain a full valence shell so they can be balanced the atoms need to lose or gain an electron.

As you can see NaCl is a fully balanced ionic compound. This process is called ionic bonding.

Data collection using a story completion task

In a story completion task, students complete a story from a "story stem", write a story from a "story cue" or suggest next steps to improve a student answer. As they do so, they reveal their assumptions about:

- the topic
- how to show deeper understanding
- themselves.

Table 3.3 presents some examples of story completion tasks.

Table 3.3: Samples of story completion tasks

Kerry is trying to compare two different superhero action figures and asks a friend for help. What happens next?
Cameron and Nick are overwhelmed by all the facts and information they have collected about the forest fires in Indonesia. They need to find a strategy for making connections between the ideas. What happens next?
The class has brainstormed a list of questions for their inquiry. The teacher suggests they sort the questions according to how difficult they will be to answer. What happens next?
Elliot asks for feedback on his written work: "The sun is a star. It is an exploding ball of gas. The sun is part of the solar system. It is very bright. The sun is made up of hydrogen and helium gas." What happens next?

Data collection using bubble drawing projective

The bubble drawing projective technique prompts the participant to complete comic strip speech and thought bubbles for an imaginary interaction between themselves and another person.

The teacher researcher describes a relevant scenario such as:

- A new teacher joins the department and you are asked to explain how you use SOLO Taxonomy with your students.
- You have lots of ideas for your speech but do not know how to organise them. Ask someone to help you.

They then ask the participant to complete the speech bubble and thought bubbles (Template 3.1) in response to the following prompts:

What are you saying?   What is the other person saying?

What are you thinking?   What are they thinking?

The interviewer follows up on the drawing by asking the participant to explain their responses.

Data collection using a student learning log

Students' learning log reflections are another source of data for qualitative analysis, which work well with the SOLO approach that allows task and outcome to be at different depths of processing or different SOLO levels. In completing it, therefore, students can both know the depth of processing or level of cognitive complexity of the task they are attempting and identify the differentiated level of their learning outcome for the task. In their learning log reflection, they:

- explain why they have self-assessed their learning outcome at a particular level
- state what they see as their next steps for learning.

The learning log can be for a simple task, such as the generic description task shown in Template 3.2. Here the task is at a SOLO multistructural level (bringing in ideas) while the outcome can be at any level of SOLO. The learning log (SOLO self-assessment rubric) prompts students to reflect on their written language outcome.

If a student completes a one-task reflection in learning logs across a sequence of lessons, they can record those responses in a learning log summary (Template 3.3) and reflect on next steps for each learning intention.

The case study that follows gives an example of how a learning log can be used for a series of lessons on a topic (Table 3.4).

Template 3.1: Bubble drawing projective activity sheet

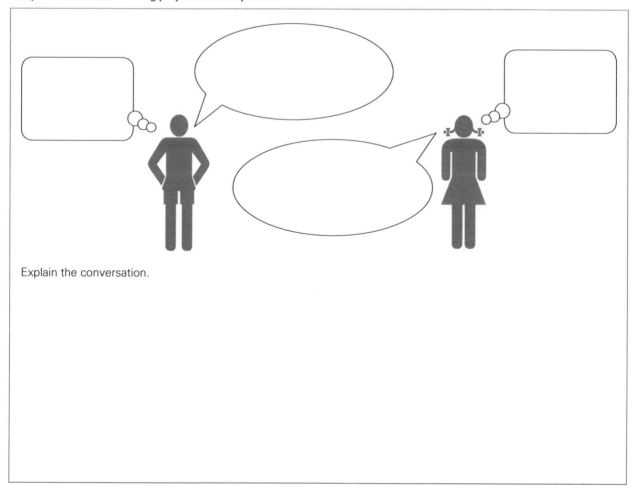

Explain the conversation.

Template 3.2: Learning log (SOLO self-assessment rubric) for a generic description task

Date	Name		
SOLO level of work (Highlight level)	**SOLO level of task**	**Describe:** Bringing in ideas **Multistructural**	
Multistructural	**Student reflection** **My work is at** _____ **level** **because**		
Relational			
Extended abstract	**My next step is to**		

- - - - - - - ✂ - ✂

Date	Name		
SOLO level of work (Highlight level)	**SOLO level of task**	**Describe:** Bringing in ideas **Multistructural**	
Multistructural	**Student reflection** **My work is at** _____ **level** **because**		
Relational			
Extended abstract	**My next step is to**		

27

Template 3.3: Learning log summary

Task 1	Task 2	Task 3	Task 4	Task 5
Learning intention _____ _____ SOLO level of task _____	Learning intention _____ _____ SOLO level of task _____	Learning intention _____ _____ SOLO level of task _____	Learning intention _____ _____ SOLO level of task _____	Learning intention _____ _____ SOLO level of task _____
Learning outcome – SOLO level Unistructural Multistructural Relational Extended abstract	Learning outcome – SOLO level Unistructural Multistructural Relational Extended abstract	Learning outcome – SOLO level Unistructural Multistructural Relational Extended abstract	Learning outcome – SOLO level Unistructural Multistructural Relational Extended abstract	Learning outcome – SOLO level Unistructural Multistructural Relational Extended abstract
My learning outcome is at _____ level because: My next step is to:	My learning outcome is at _____ level because: My next step is to:	My learning outcome is at _____ level because: My next step is to:	My learning outcome is at _____ level because: My next step is to:	My learning outcome is at _____ level because: My next step is to:

Overall reflection on learning:

Data analysis

To decide on the best codes to analyse the data, the teacher researcher reads the text multiple times. They may decide to base their codes on:

- events in the order they happen, noting them as events or critical incidents, turning points or "aha" moments
- storyline in terms of characters, settings, problem, action and resolution
- themes
- use of effort and/or learning strategy (frequency), type of use (directed, supported, independent) and context for use (flexibility).

Case study: Using thematic analysis to study depth of process

It is widely understood that students sit somewhere on a continuum of approaches to learning and learning depth: from surface learning that involves approaches such as a memorising (reproductive) strategy to deep learning with organising approaches that focus on finding relationships and connections through reformulating and understanding information (Saljo 1981; Watkins 1983). Earlier studies have shown that the approach they use seems to have significant consequences for what they learn rather than for how much they learn (Saljo 1981).

Further study is needed on the nature of the differences between approaches, the origin of such differences, and their practical implications in various learning contexts. Saljo (1981, p 69) also found a theoretically and conceptually interesting parallel between the kinds of learning students engage in and their own descriptions of their approach. This study points to the importance of the depth of students' approach to learning. Correlating its findings with those from studies on the impact of the quality of the learning outcomes could be an area for further research. When the SOLO and depth categories were cross-classified, a strong relationship was found between depth of processing and the quality of learning outcomes.

Compelling evidence shows that the quality of the specific learning outcomes has an impact on student learning. High-quality learning outcomes have been associated with deep approaches to learning, and low-quality learning outcomes with surface approaches (Boulton-Lewis et al 2001). When learning outcomes are classified at a higher SOLO level, they lead to a deeper level of learning for students, as judged from students' explanations of a learning task they have worked on recently in class. Such findings have implications for supporting students to develop and demonstrate learning to appropriate SOLO levels, and engage in effective learning strategies for successful academic outcomes (Watkins 1983).

Responding to the need for further understanding in this area, this empirical study examined the impact of well-structured learning outcomes on a student's ability to determine their level of understanding for a particular concept.

The sample

This case study involves a top-band Year 10 girls' science class. Students had been taught about atomic structure, electron configuration and formation of ions during the year. The study was completed during review of students' examination answers, where students were given the learning log to reflect their level of understanding, which allowed the teacher researcher to investigate the relationship between depth of processing and the quality of learning outcomes.

The task

Individually the students were instructed:

1. Have a look at the old version of the learning outcomes and then at the new version.
2. Read your exam answer.
3. Go to the following link and complete the survey (link provided).

Learning outcomes

The following was the original version of the learning outcomes:

1. Write electron arrangements for atoms and their ions.
2. Explain why atoms form ions and determine the charge on ions using electron arrangements.
3. Understand simple ionic bonding.
4. Write simple balanced formulas, and name ions including Cl^-, O^{2-}, S^{2-}, Na^+, K^+, H^+, Ca^{2+}, Mg^{2+}, Al^{3+}, N^{3-}, I^-.

In a new approach, the students were presented with the learning outcomes within the broader framework of a learning log, which set out success criteria associated with each one (Table 3.4).

Table 3.4: Example of a learning log for Year 10 science – chemical reactions

Chemical reactions	Multistructural	Relational	Extended abstract
Learning intention	**Success criteria**		
Write electron arrangements for atoms and their ions.	Identify the number of electrons in an atom structure from the atomic number. • The number of protons = the number of electrons in an atom.	Describe the number of electrons in an atom structure from the atomic number and the number of electrons in each shell. • The maximum number of electrons in each shell = 2,8,8.	Compare the number of electrons and electron configuration of an atom and its ion. • Negative ions form when an atom gains electrons. They have more electrons than protons. • Positive ions form when an atom loses electrons. They have fewer electrons than protons.
My learning outcome is at level _____ because: My next step is to:			
Explain why atoms form ions and determine the charge on ions using electron arrangements.	Define an ion as an atom that has gained or lost an electron during a chemical reaction. • Metals lose valence electrons to form positive ions. • Non-metals gain valence electrons to form negative ions.	Explain that atoms lose or gain electrons during a chemical reaction to become stable. • Metals lose valence electrons in order to have a complete valence shell and become more stable. Metals form positive ions. • Non-metals gain valence electrons in order to have a complete valence shell and become more stable. Non-metals form negative ions.	Discuss why atoms form positive and negative ions when they lose and gain valence electrons respectively. • Metals lose valence electrons in order to have a complete valence shell and become more stable. Metals form positive ions because when valence electrons are lost, there are more positive protons in the nucleus than there are electrons in the electron shells. • Non-metals gain valence electrons in order to have a complete valence shell and become more stable. Non-metals form negative ions because when valence electrons are gained, there are more negative electrons in the electron shells than there are protons in the nucleus.
My learning outcome is at level _____ because: My next step is to:			

continued ...

Table 3.4: Example of a learning log for Year 10 science – chemical reactions (continued)

Learning intention	Success criteria		
Understand simple ionic bonding.	Describe ionic bonds as bonds that form between metal atoms and non-metal atoms.	Explain what an ionic bond is. • Ionic bonds are bonds that form between metal atoms and non-metal atoms when valence electrons are transferred from the metal atom to the non-metal atom.	Discuss the difference between a positive ion and a negative ion and link how they form to give a formula that is 1:1 and 1:2. • Ionic bonds are bonds that form between metal atoms and non-metal atoms. • During a chemical reaction, metal atoms donate valence electrons to a non-metal atom. • The respective charge of the ions formed depends on the number of valence electrons that are lost or gained. • The ionic bonds that form during this process are electronically neutral – they have no charge.

My learning outcome is at level _____ because:

My next step is to:

Write simple balanced formulas, and name ions including Cl^-, O^{2-}, S^{2-}, Na^+, K^+, H^+, Ca^{2+}, Mg^{2+}, Al^{3+}, N^{3-}, I^-.	Can write a formula for an ionic substance made up of +1 and –1 ions.	Can write a formula for an ionic substance made up of +2 and –2 ions.	Can write a formula for an ionic substance made up of +1 and –2 ions or +2 and –1 ions.

My learning outcome is at level _____ because:

My next step is to:

Overall assessment of my confidence in my ability to do the following:

• **Multistructural task:** Identify the number of electrons in an atom structure from the atomic number. Define an ion as an atom that has gained or lost an electron during a chemical reaction. Describe ionic bonds as bonds that form between metal atoms and non-metal atoms. Write a formula for an ionic substance made up of +1 and –1 ions.

Student reflection:

• **Relational task:** Describe the number of electrons in an atom structure from the atomic number and the number of electrons in each shell. Explain that atoms lose or gain electrons during a chemical reaction to become stable. Explain what an ionic bond is. Write a formula for an ionic substance made up of +2 and –2 ions.

Student reflection:

• **Extended abstract task:** Compare the number of electrons and electron configuration of an atom and its ion. Discuss why atoms form positive and negative ions when they lose and gain valence electrons respectively. Discuss the difference between a positive ion and a negative ion and link how they form to give a formula that is 1:1 and 1:2. Write a formula for an ionic substance made up of +1 and –2 ions or +2 and –1 ions.

Student reflection:

The inquiry outcome

Figure 3.4 presents samples of work that three students produced through this process. Each of these students also responded to a survey on this unit of work, as recorded in Table 3.5. The thematic analysis showed that, when using the old version of the learning outcomes, the students differed in their view as to which of the learning outcomes was being assessed. In contrast, all three students found the more detailed version of the learning outcomes more informative about their level of learning as it helped them to understand what they needed to do to provide an extended abstract answer. Each student was able to identify what they could add to their exam answer to take it to a deeper level of thinking.

With the restructured learning outcomes, therefore, the students could identify where they were missing information in their answers and what they needed to do to reach the next SOLO level.

Figure 3.4: Examples of Year 10 chemistry student responses to examination question

Student (a)

Material World

Question one: Atoms, Acids and Bases

a) Complete the following table using your table of ions and periodic table.

Symbol	Number of protons	Number of electrons	Number of neutrons	Mass number	Arrangement of electrons
Na^+	11	11	12	23	2, 8, 1
Mg^{2+}	12	12	12	24	2, 8, 2
O^{2-}	8	10	8	16	2, 6

b) Discuss why magnesium chloride has the formula $MgCl_2$ whereas sodium chloride has the formula NaCl. In your answer, include:

- **The charges of the ions that make up each compound**
- **The ratio of atoms**
- **The overall charge of each compound**

Magnesium chloride has the formula of $MgCl_2$ as this is the balanced formula. The magnesium ion is Mg^{2+} and the chloride ion is Cl^-. To make these balanced we must add another chloride ion. This is then balanced and the formula is just how many ions of each are needed for balance. In this case it is 1 magnesium and 2 chloride so the formula is $MgCl_2$. For sodium chloride the sodium ion is Na^+ and the chloride ion is Cl^- so in this case no more ions are needed to make it balanced, just one of each. This means the formula is NaCl. The overall charges of NaCl and $MgCl_2$ are ~~not~~ neutral.

continued ...

Student (b)

Mg stands for magnesium, and Na stands for sodium. Cl stands for chloride.

At the start, each ion is either positively or negatively charged. Magnesium ion was Mg²⁺, which means it gained 2 electrons to become stable and negatively charged. Two of Cl is needed as to balance out the Mg²⁺, resulting in a neutral ionic compound. Because sodium and chloride are both charged with 1 electron, they only need each other to form a neutral ionic compound. One atom gains electrons to form a full valence shell while the other atom loses electrons to do the same.

Student (c)

If the Magnesium has 12 electrons and chlorine has 17 so the electron configuration for magnesium is 2,8,2 and the electron configuration for chlorine is 2,8,7 Magnesium and chlorine join together to form an ionic compound although there is a 2 which represent electrons, these will either need to be gained or lost. Whereas with sodium chloride the two completely cancel each other out as they would have needed what the other had. The atoms need to gain or lose electron or order to gain a full valence shell so they can be well balanced. Mg²⁺ + Cl⁻ → MgCl₂ this is because you switch around the electrons. Na⁺ + Cl⁻ → NaCl, as you can see sodium chloride is a fully balanced ionic compound. This process is called ionic bonding.

Table 3.5: Student views on two versions of learning outcomes in relation to their answers to an examination question (Figure 3.4)

Student (a)	Student (b)	Student (c)
Read your examination question. Can you identify which of the old learning outcomes it is written to examine? If so, which one(s)?		
Explain why atoms form ions and determine the charge on ions using electron arrangements.	Understand simple ionic bonding.	Understand simple ionic bonding.
Have a look at the new structured learning outcomes. Does this structure give you more information about how you need to answer your examination question?		
Yes	Yes	Yes
If the new structured learning outcomes give you more information about how you need to answer your examination question, how does it help?		
It helps by proving what is needed to write an extended abstract answer.	This helps because it is more specific in what is expected. It tells you exactly what is being asked of you and goes into detail. It also shows you what level you will be achieving at in relation to what you include in your answer.	It has the key facts included in the learning outcomes that we read over and over again so it helps when trying to remember the most important pieces of information as well as the mark.
Using the new structured learning outcomes, what level of achievement do you think your answer is at?		
Relational, maybe extended abstract but my answers are off.	Merit/relational	Relational
Using the new structured learning outcomes, what would you add to your examination answer? Please note down what you would add to your answer.		
The difference between metals and non-metals, the ratio of atoms (?)	I would go into more depth about what an ionic bond is, I would also try elaborate on why atoms form ions and I would also try explain more of the differences between negative and positively charged electrons and when they become negatively charged or positively charged.	I would add the phrase valence shells and valence electrons as I forgot to use the proper and correct wording for the outer shell and the difference between positive and negative ions.
How could you use the new structured learning outcomes to inform you of your learning?		
When writing practice answers, to check back and make sure I've covered all there is for an extended abstract answer.	The new learning outcomes help more as they are more specific and you can also see what you would need to do in order to achieve at a higher level.	It is easy to point out the things that I do know and the things that I may need to have another look at to fully understand.

continued ...

Table 3.5: Student views on two versions of learning outcomes in relation to their answers to an examination question (Figure 3.4) (continued)

Which of the learning outcomes, old or new, would help you measure what you already know?		
Write simple balanced formula, and name ions including Cl⁻, O²⁻, S²⁻, Na⁺, K⁺, H⁺, Ca²⁺, Mg²⁺, Al³⁺, N³⁻, I⁻ Because of all the learning outcomes, balanced formulas is what I understand the best. Therefore, I can use it to measure what I already know.	The new learning outcomes, as they are much more specific and state more than one thing.	I think the old learning outcomes measure what I already know because they are short sentences which can be quite vague so I will only tick it off when studying if I know exactly what they mean.
Which of the learning outcomes, old or new, would help you measure changes in your learning over time?		
New, in particular; Explain why atoms form ions and determine the charge on ions using electron arrangements, and understand simple ionic bonding. Both of these I am still not the most confident about, so over time as I create a deeper understanding I can use them to make sure I have then studied everything.	The new learning outcomes would help me more. As it also shows you what you would need to add in order to get a higher grade.	New because when studying they make you go back and look through notes to find exactly what they learning outcome is and study it. They also show the depth you need to go into the achieve at the different levels for each outcome.

Note: All three students were given a grade of M+ (upper Merit) for their work presented in Figure 3.4.

Interpretative phenomenological analysis

In **interpretative phenomenological analysis**, the teacher researcher is interested in how the student (or a teaching colleague) makes sense of their lived experiences using SOLO.

The teacher researcher looks at what the participant experienced and how this individual experienced or saw it. They may also look for commonalities in how participants talk about or describe the use of SOLO in teaching and learning.

The research approach explores the experience of the student in the context of their classroom and school environment and the meanings they attach to these experiences.

Comparative studies can be made either over time (before and after) or between different groups. The sample size is usually small, comprising one to six participants who share a similar experience or context.

Using interpretative phenomenological analysis, we can ask how students make sense of learning and strive to see learning through the eyes of the students themselves. We can work to understand how students' own views change as they transition from seeing learning as something they do when directed to seeing it as something you plan, monitor and evaluate using SOLO as your own mental model, when you are "being a learner".

On the following pages, we briefly outline a method of collecting and analysing your data when conducting interpretative phenomenological analysis. A case study then illustrates the use of this approach.

Data collection using an in-depth interview

For interpretative phenomenological analysis, an effective interview is in-depth, semi-structured and conducted face to face. Questions should explore the focus of the teacher inquiry. Once you have come up with an initial list of questions, try them out in pilot interviews so that you can refine and develop them to be relevant and easy to understand. Template 3.4 sets out an interview guide that can be used to explore students' views of SOLO as a model of learning.

Template 3.4: In-depth interview guide for exploring students' views of SOLO as a model of learning

Interview focus: Student responses to the introduction of SOLO as a model of learning
Time:
Place:
Interviewer:
Student (year level):
Questions 1. How did you first learn about SOLO? 2. What happened afterwards? 3. Can you tell me about a time when you used SOLO with your learning in school? 4. Can you tell me about a time when you used SOLO with your learning outside of school? 5. What difference has SOLO made to your learning? 6. Would you recommend SOLO to other students? 7. What are the best things about using SOLO in your learning? 8. What are the problems with using SOLO in your learning? 9. Who should I talk with to find out more about using SOLO?

Data analysis

The following approach is adapted from Creswell (2013), who provides a useful framework for teachers analysing phenomenological data.

1. Write a full description of your own experience of using SOLO in the classroom. In this way, you can identify your own perspectives as the teacher researcher and hold them separate from the views of your participants.

2. Read and re-read the participants' narratives and pull out statements of significance. It can help to record each one on a separate Post-it note, which helps you to treat them all as having equal importance.

3. Make a selection of stand-alone, non-overlapping statements.

4. Organise the statements into larger groups (clusters or clumps) on the basis of their shared features. It can be easier to unpack broader themes if you ask what each clump of statements represents or is an example of.

5. Write three descriptions of the participants' experience: textural – what happened, with examples; structural – how it happened; and composite – capturing both the "what" and the "how" and analysing the data for themes (Table 3.6).

Table 3.6: Three descriptions of participants' experience as explored through interpretative phenomenological analysis

Textural description	Structural description	Composite description
Describe "what" happened – including examples	Describe "how" it happened – setting and context	**Essence of the experience** Describe "what" happened and "how" it happened

Case study: Using interpretative phenomenological analysis

This case study presents a teacher inquiry on students' experiences of SOLO tasks and learning outcomes, which made use of interpretative phenomenological analysis. HOT SOLO maps and rubrics were prepared for the learning outcomes listed under "The task" below.

The sample

This case study involves a co-educational Year 13 (NCEA Level 3) chemistry class of mixed ability.

The task

In groups, students broke down the different components that determine the different isomers found in organic chemistry.

Learning outcomes (for Achievement Standard 3.5) were to:

- distinguish between structural isomerism and stereoisomerism (geometric and optical) (see Table 3.7)
- draw and name isomers of organic compounds of up to eight carbon atoms.

Figure 3.5 shows the adapted HookED SOLO Describe++ map students used to complete this task. Levels of achievement for these learning outcomes in the end-of-topic test were compared with those for the other learning outcomes.

Table 3.7: Example of a learning log for Year 13 science – organic chemistry

Organic chemistry	Multistructural	Relational	Extended abstract
Learning intention	**Success criteria**		
Distinguish between structural isomerism and stereoisomerism (geometric and optical).	Define a structural isomer, a geometric isomer and an optical isomer. • Structural isomers have the same molecular formula but the atoms are arranged differently. • A geometric isomer has to have a C=C with different groups bonded to each of the C in the double bond. • Optical isomers exist for molecules containing a carbon atom with 4 different groups attached.	Compare a structural isomer, geometric isomer and optical isomers. • Structural isomers will have different shapes because the atoms in the molecule are arranged differently. • Geometric cis/trans isomers have restricted rotation around the C=C, and different groups bonded to each C in the C=C. This enables cis/trans isomers to form. • Optical isomers exist for molecules containing a carbon atom with 4 different groups attached. This carbon is called a chiral C. These groups in the optical isomers are arranged differently in 3D space around the chiral C.	Link the structure of structural isomers, geometric isomers and optical isomers to a physical property that can be used to distinguish them. • Structural isomers have different physical properties because their structures have a different shape or in some cases a different functional group, so the intermolecular forces have different strengths. • Geometric isomers have different physical properties due to the shape of the cis/trans molecule about the C=C. The difference in shape leads to a difference in the way the molecules are able to interact with themselves, therefore geometric isomers will have differing intermolecular force strengths. • Optical isomers have the same physical properties, but will rotate plane-polarised light in opposite directions. • If the one of the optical isomers is biologically active, the other optical isomer will not be biologically active.

Figure 3.5: Adapted HookED SOLO Describe++ map for Year 13 organic chemistry task on isomers

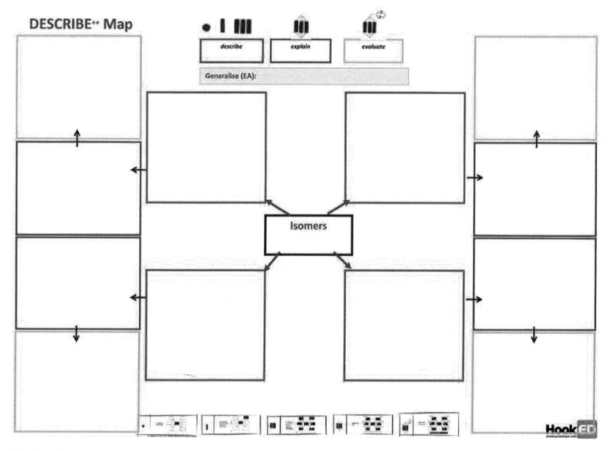

The inquiry outcomes

Students were interviewed with the task in front of them. They were asked to describe what the task was and how it differed from other types of tasks they had done, and then relate the task to how it helped them learn.

Through interpretative phenomenological analysis, the teacher researcher identified common themes from the interview transcripts. In particular, students said that using the SOLO map helped them to:

- structure an answer
- identify the details that need to go into an answer
- relate all of their ideas about isomers in a structured way.

The following are some of the comments students made:

> This mind map helps me plot a path. I start by describing the ideas. Listing the definitions. Then I go to the next box and I kind of explain what those ideas are, and then in the third box I link the ideas back to the question. (Year 13 chemistry student)

> The boxes really help to know how to structure an answer and how to push up a grade boundary. (Year 13 chemistry student)

4. Using numbers as evidence – quantitative data

When teachers use numbers as evidence, their teacher inquiry goes further than description. By using a quantitative approach, they can visualise their data and identify the extent of a change in student learning outcomes.

This section begins with some quick tips for visualising and interpreting quantitative data. It then examines two aspects of a quantitative approach in more depth – analysing for effect size; and collecting and analysing evidence through randomised controlled trials – with a strong emphasis on case studies.

Quick tips for visualising and interpreting quantitative data

Using graphs to present your data is a useful first step to visualise your information on student learning. An easy way to graph the data is to plot student outcome versus frequency. The shape of the graph will give you a sense of grouped or spread student data, high and low values, clusters of data and/or outliers (that is, one-off results that are much higher or lower than your general findings).

Calculating the **mean** is a simple calculation you can do to find out the average size of any change in the learning outcome that has occurred following the intervention. Here you add all the numbers together and divide by the number of participants in the sample.

It is also helpful to get an idea of the spread of the data. To do this, you can:

* look at your graph to identify the **range** – the lowest and highest outcomes in the student sample
* calculate the **standard deviation** to measure the average spread of the data from the mean. It is especially useful when trying to determine effect size of an intervention on the student learning outcome (see below).

Effect size

Two questions at first glance seem very similar:

* Did the intervention change the learning outcome?
* How much did the intervention change the learning outcome?

However, in a context where every intervention can change the learning outcome, the answer to the first is of little consequence when making decisions about pedagogical next steps. The answer to the second matters, because if we know the extent of change we can discriminate between desired change and simple teacher effects.

For example, imagine that, in a five-week teacher inquiry, the teacher introduced the use of SOLO maps and self-assessment rubrics to help students draft ideas for their writing tasks. At the end of the five weeks, students write on a previously unseen topic. The SOLO mapping writing samples have an average score of 85, compared with 77 before the intervention. The SOLO maps intervention certainly changed the learning outcome, but we need a reliable and consistent measure of the extent of the change to find out if it is a change that matters.

Calculating the effect size of an intervention used in a teacher inquiry is an easy way to get an indication of how much the intervention changed the student learning outcome.

The **effect-size method** is a simple way teachers can calculate the effect of an intervention on student outcomes. With this method, we can compare the average pre- and post-test results to identify the effect of the intervention:

* *within* a cohort of students – comparing their results *before and after* the research intervention (**effect size within a cohort**) or
* *between* treatment groups and controls – such as comparing a sample of students who experience the intervention with another group of students who do not (**effect sizes between cohorts**).

The result (effect size) is expressed in units of **standard deviation** (a measure of the spread from the mean).[1] It asks how many standard deviations separate the control group mean from the experimental group mean.

Effect size (*d*) = Average (post-test) − Average (pre-test) / Spread (standard deviation)

The difference between the two means is divided by the measure of spread (standard deviation) of the control group. So the effect size is the mean difference between the two groups expressed in standard deviation units. The smaller the effect size, the closer (more similar) the means of the two groups being compared.

As Hattie (2009, pp 7–8) describes it:

> An effect-size of *d* = 1.0 indicates an increase of one standard deviation. A one standard deviation increase is typically associated with advancing children's achievement by two to three years, improving the rate of learning by 50%, or a correlation between some variable (e.g., amount of homework) and achievement of approximately *r* = 0.50. When implementing a new program, an effect-size of 1.0 would mean that, on average, students receiving that treatment would exceed 84% of students not receiving that treatment.

Table 4.1 summarises Hattie's explanation.

Table 4.1: How to interpret an effect size of *d* = 1.0

If your teacher inquiry data shows an effect size *d* = 1.0, then this represents …			
… an increase of	… an advance in achievement by	… an improvement in the rate of learning by	… a correlation of
one standard deviation	two to three years	50%	approximately *r* = 0.50

Source: Based on Hattie (2009)

The **hinge point** (effect-size norm) is useful for determining the effectiveness of an intervention because every intervention will have some effect on learning (see Table 4.2). As Hattie (2009, pp 7–8) describes it, any intervention with an effect size that is greater than the norm (0.4) is creating more than expected growth in the outcome that is being targeted.

Table 4.2: How to interpret different effect sizes

Effect size (*d*)	Is evidence of …
Below 0.0	Detrimental effects
0.0 to 0.5	Developmental effects
0.2 to 0.4	Teacher effects
Above 0.4	Desired effects – the positive result of the intervention

Effect-size research also identifies students who progress differently from their peers, allowing teacher researchers to explore reasons for these differences and to use this information in determining next steps in teaching.

If you find variance, spread, mean and standard deviation are challenging, you can set up an Excel spreadsheet to help you. The essential steps here are to:

1. create a data table for the sample group (before the intervention or without the treatment)
2. calculate the mean result for the group
3. use these data to calculate the standard deviation or spread of the data (square root of the variance)
4. create a data table for the experimental group (after the treatment)
5. calculate the difference between the two means

---

1   In a normal distribution, 68 per cent of values lie within a band around the mean with a width of one standard deviation.

6. divide this difference by the measure of spread (standard deviation) of the sample group to calculate the effect size of the intervention.

If a teacher inquiry showed an effect size of greater than 0.4, it would be worthwhile attempting to replicate it with another cohort of students.

For further explanation of effect sizes, using worked examples, see Hattie (2009, p 8; 2012, Appendix E).

Case study: Effect size of using SOLO Taxonomy in science

This case study is from Clifton Community School, a community arts school in Rotherham, England. Its purpose was to quantify the long-term impact of SOLO Taxonomy on science learning.

School context

Clifton is a secondary school of over 1000 students. Its wider community faces substantial challenges in the form of persistent high unemployment, high socioeconomic deprivation and low aspirations among parents and students, which began with the forced decline of the coal and steel industries in the 1980s.

The composition of the student intake brings additional challenges, notably:

- almost 60 per cent of students receive free school meals due to high socioeconomic deprivation
- over 30 per cent of students speak English as a second language
- a quarter of all students have a diagnosed special educational need
- the mobility of students is high.

On a nationwide basis, Clifton is among the top quarter of schools facing challenges as defined by the highest percentages in each of these measures.

Recent government reforms to the education system have produced rapid and unpredictable changes, with the result that the school went into decline. In 2014 it was placed in "Special Measures" by government inspectors; the school was graded "inadequate" against all judgements (overall effectiveness, leadership and management, behaviour and safety of students, quality of teaching and achievement of students).

Clifton Science embraces SOLO

In 2012 the Clifton Science team introduced SOLO Taxonomy into its curriculum, with a view to combating stagnating progress, improving depth of learning and maintaining a focus on learning despite the external turbulence. SOLO was initially embedded in long-, medium- and short-term planning to challenge all students at every point in every lesson. Weekly staff development was also used to embed SOLO into teacher skills such as questioning.

The initial focus was on Years 9–11 (ages 14–16 years). The goal was to improve performance in Year 11 external examinations, which would allow them to access a higher level of courses when they went on to college.

Research focus

In the United Kingdom, students sit external examinations in Year 6 (before they go to secondary school) and Year 11 (before they go to college). Clifton Science could therefore identify the effect size of introducing SOLO with a high degree of confidence. By using these assessments, the team could also gather information about the full breadth of the curriculum to be assessed.

Unfortunately, it was only possible to do this for students studying "academic" courses. "Vocational" courses were subject to government intervention and changing in many substantial ways at the time of the research, so it would not have been possible to measure the impact of SOLO alone on outcomes from these courses.

Learning outcomes

Table 4.3 presents the effect sizes found through the data analysis.

Thus despite the somewhat turbulent environment within the school and education systems, the effect size is higher than at least 118 of the 138 strategies originally identified by Hattie (2009). Furthermore, the effect sizes are likely to be underestimates as this year group only followed a SOLO curriculum for their final three years at Clifton.

Table 4.3: Effect sizes of introducing SOLO Taxonomy to science classes at Clifton Community School

Student group	Effect size	
	Over five years	Average per year
2015 cohort	3.14	0.63
High-attaining students	3.76	0.75
Middle-attaining students	3.03	0.61

Just as pleasing is that in 2014 students' outcomes were in the top 10 per cent in the United Kingdom. A similar number is expected for 2015 despite a much higher proportion studying academic science subjects. Indeed, from 2016 onwards all students will study academic science courses at Clifton.

Finally, an increased percentage of students is now achieving grade C or higher in academic science qualifications (Table 4.4). In real terms, this level of progress meant that the number of Clifton students who could access the most challenging courses at college increased by 13 per cent from 2013 to 2015.

Table 4.4: Percentage of science students achieving grade C or higher after introducing SOLO Taxonomy to science classes at Clifton Community School

Year	Number of years of SOLO curriculum	Percentage achieving grade C or higher
2013	1	34%
2014	2	36%
2015	3	47%

Randomised controlled trials

In a randomised controlled trial, a teacher researcher randomly assigns individuals to an intervention group or a control group. They then compare the data on the progress of each group, such as data on student outcomes for a group using SOLO Taxonomy compared with student outcomes for a group that does not use SOLO.

The following case studies illustrate this approach in the context of drama and science classes at St Kentigern College.

Case study: Using randomised controlled trials to compare drama classes

The sample

Two Year 11 drama classes completed the same internal assessment but one class was taught completely with a SOLO structure while the other was not.

The tasks

The SOLO-related tasks for the SOLO class were as follows:

1. Before teaching began, the teacher unpacked the internal assessment with students and linked SOLO verbs to the different outcomes.
2. Students peer-assessed each other using a SOLO rubric as the internal assessment progressed, and reflected on the SOLO level of the answers with the class. This assessment was then linked directly to NCEA outcomes.

The inquiry outcomes

By unpacking the internal standard using the SOLO rubric, students in the SOLO class were able to peer-assess each other's work throughout the internal assessment and give valid feedback (Figure 4.1). Having the learning structured in this way deepened students' understanding, as demonstrated by the effect size calculated based on the internal assessment. For the SOLO class, working with the SOLO-structured learning outcomes, the effect size was 0.55, compared with 0.317 for the class that learnt with conventional learning outcomes (Table 4.5).

Student (a)

Performance Success Criteria **Devising**			The Devising Process /cycle	Written evidence - what's involved? Two aspects	
Unit title: Devise And Perform A Drama to Realise An Intention			What preparation work do I need to do?	Statement of Intention	Script on
Achieved	Achieved with Merit	Achieved with Excellence			
	• Devise And Perform A Drama To Realise An Intention.	• Devise And Perform A Coherent Drama To Realise An Intention		• The Rationale For The Devised Drama • The Style of The Devised Drama	• A Title • A List of Characters • A Script or A Devised Drama Outline
Explain the meaning of 'a drama to realise an intention'		• Devise And Perform An Effective Drama To Realise An Intention		• If Necessary, Decisions About Staging & Use of Technology	• Decisions About The Drama elements
Given Example	Look at Explanatory Notes Highlight all points needed for Merit	Look at Explanatory Notes Highlight all points needed for Excellence			
				Vocab list	Meaning & example
Identify key words in Excellence		Example and meaning	List ideas on how I can prove I have been involved in this cycle		
Effective				Role	
Emotion				Time	
Radiance				Place	
Tension				Tension	
Structer				mood	

continued ...

Student (b)

Performance Success Criteria: Devising			The Devising Process /cycle	Written evidence – what's involved? Two aspects	
Unit title: Devise and perform a drama to realise our intention AS91214			What preparation work do I need to do (meets with group, brainstorming)	Statement of Intention	Script on Outline
Achieved	Achieved with Merit	Achieved with Excellence		• the rationale for the devised drama • the style of the devised drama • if necessary, decisions about staging and use of techniques	• a title • list of characters • a script or devised drama outline • decisions about the drama elements • conventions that are used and why
Devise and perform a drama to realise an intention	Devise, explement and perform a coherent drama to realise an intention	Devise and perform an effective drama to realise an intention			
Explain the meaning of "a drama to realise an intention" a drama that conveys a message and gets to a point or story that they wish to tell.	Look at Explanatory Notes Highlight all points needed for Merit • coherent • Devise a coherent drama conveys meaning, actions that ... structured to have flow, dramatic unity, and smooth transitions between scenes.	Look at Explanatory Notes Highlight all points needed for Excellence • effective • Devise an effective drama conveys meaning, actions that is convincing, original. the essence of the ... can contain/has impact and Originality.			
Give an Example that the intention is to make an issue, the issue should be made by the end of the piece.		Perform/devise to present the drama as devised. The Performs is a what to convey the effectiveness of the drama.			
Identify key words in Excellence		Example and meaning	List ideas on how I can prove I have been involved in this cycle	Vocab list	Meaning & example
Effective		Successful in producing a desired or intended result.	Keep record of ideas discussed	Rationale	Why the rationale
Convincing		Capable of causing someone to believe something is true or real.	Note down each time the group is working together	decisions	what is decided for what reasons
Originality		The quality of being unusual. Also the ability to think independently than other ideas.	Keep a diary / checklist	Structure	the foundation, flow and Base for the drama follows
Impact		To have strong force or effect on someone or something.	Come to everyclass	Intention	what is needed or an intention. Why you want
Performance		The act of presenting a task or play, concert, or other form of entertainment.	Know what is going on within my group	Conventions	the conventions used in the performance

44

Table 4.5: Effect sizes of SOLO drama class compared with non-SOLO drama class in randomised controlled trial

Drama class	Effect size	Assessment of effect size (based on Hattie, 2012)
SOLO class	0.55	Falls in the zone of desired effect
Non-SOLO class	0.317	Falls in the zone of teacher effects

Case study: Using randomised controlled trials with a Year 10 science class

The sample

Year 10 science students (a middle-band girls' class) had been taught about acids and bases during the year, using the learning outcomes as set out in Table 4.6. The class average grade for this topic after this teaching was A4. A random sample of these students was taken to participate in an inquiry completed during a revision session before the end-of-year examination.

Table 4.6: Original learning outcomes (pre-SOLO intervention) for chemical reactions

Learning outcome	Overall assessment of my confidence to be able to answer questions on … Give an example of an answer.
Define the pH scale	
Use indicators to measure pH (universal indicator, litmus paper)	
Recognise a neutralisation reaction and write a word equation for it	
Explain what happens at a chemical level during neutralisation	

The tasks

In groups, students worked through the following tasks, framed in terms of SOLO Taxonomy, to achieve the learning outcomes as listed in Table 4.6 above.

Task 1: Students were to list all that they knew about the science behind each learning outcome and place these ideas under the heading *Multistructural*. From there they looked for components from their list that were related to each other and were asked to create a mind map under *Relational* to show how the concepts linked. Finally students defined the pH scale, using all of their relational knowledge, to construct an extended abstract answer and record it under the *Extended abstract* heading (Figure 4.2).

Task 2: Students recorded their Task 1 ideas on SOLO hexagons and arranged them to show the relationships among them (Figure 4.3). They then talked through their thinking behind their placement of the hexagons.

Task 3: Students were given a learning log in which the learning outcomes were extended to include success criteria, coded by SOLO level. In a self-assessment, students used the learning log to identify the SOLO level they had achieved for each of the learning outcomes. Table 4.7 presents the part of the learning log that related to "Define the pH scale"; a similar approach was taken with the other three learning outcomes.

Follow-up test: Students completed an Excellence-styled practice question about acid–base neutralisation. Figure 4.4 presents two examples of student answers: one graded M5 (lower Merit) and the other E7 (lower Excellence).

Define the pH Scale

Wednesday, 11 November 2015   3.47 p.m.

Multistructural

- acids are sour
- bases are soapy
- pH is a measure of how acid or basic it is
- pH 1 = acid - red
  pH 14 = basic - purple
- red, orange, yellow, green, blue, purple
- an acid and base react together and neutralise eachother
- acids have H^+ ions
- bases have OH^- ions
- pH = 7 = neutral
- neutral = $H^+ = OH^-$

Relational

- pH is a measure of how acid or base a substance is

↓

pH 1 = acid, pH 7 = neutral and pH 14 = base.

↓

pH 1 acids have lots of H^+ ions / few OH^- and pH 14 have lots of OH^- ions. / few H^+ ions.

↓

When H^+ and OH^- are equal the solution pH = 7 and it will be neutral.

Extended abstract

The pH scale is a measure of how much H^+ there is in a solution.

When there is lots of H^+, the solution has a low pH and is acidic. - not much OH^-.

As the pH scale value increases, the amount of H^+ ion decreases and the amount OH^- begins to increase

When $H^+ = OH^-$ the pH = 7 and the solution is neutral

At the far end of the pH scale - pH 14 there is lots of OH^- and very little H^+. The solution with a pH = 14 is basic

46

Figure 4.3: Example of using SOLO hexagons to show relationships among ideas related to the learning outcome "Define the pH scale"

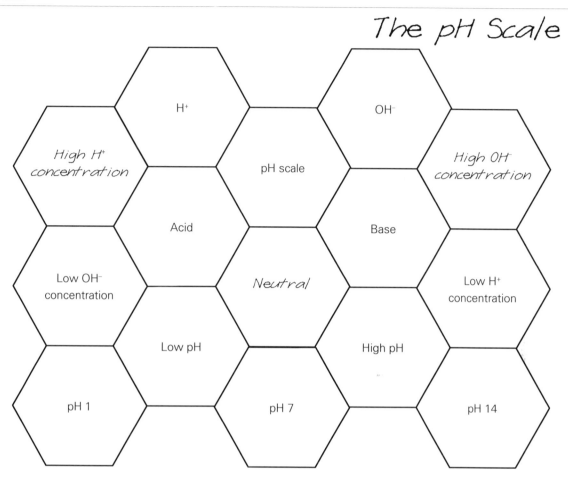

Table 4.7: Learning log for self-assessment of SOLO level for each learning outcome on chemical reactions

Chemical reactions	Multistructural	Relational	Extended abstract
Learning intention	**Success criteria**		
Define the pH scale	Describe the pH scale as being a measure of acidity from pH level 1–14. • Identify the following levels: pH 1 is strong acid pH 7 is neutral pH 14 is strong alkali	Describe *how* a solution's pH can be used to determine which solution is more acidic or more alkali. • Identify that acids have an excess H+ ion in solution and bases have an excess OH− ion concentration in solution.	Compare and contrast pH and concentration of H+ and OH− • The lower the pH, the higher the H+ concentration and the lower the OH− concentration. • The higher the pH, the lower the H+ concentration and the higher the OH− concentration.

My learning outcome is at level _____ because:

My next step is to:

Student (a)

Year 10 Acids and Bases – Practice Question

M 5

Question 1

A student has three unlabelled beakers each containing a colourless liquid. One contains **water**, one contains a solution of **sodium carbonate**, and one contains **Hydrochloric acid**. To work out which liquid is which, the student put a drop from each beaker onto a piece of blue litmus paper and a piece of red litmus paper. She then added universal indicator to each beaker.

	Colour of blue litmus	Colour of red litmus	Colour of universal indicator	Name of the liquid
Beaker 1	Stays blue	Stays red	Turns green	Water neutral ph 7
Beaker 2	Turns red	Stays red	Turns red	Acid m7-6 A Hydrochloric acid
Beaker 3	Stays blue	Turns blue	Turns blue	Sodium carbonate

Question 2

A beaker contains sodium hydroxide solution and 5 drops of universal indicator. hydrochloric acid was added to the beaker until no more changes were observed.

(a) Write a word equation for the reaction between hydrochloric acid and sodium hydroxide.

Sodium hydroxide + hydrochloric acid ⟶ Sodium chloride + Water

(b) Describe how the indicator colour changes as the hydrochloric acid is added to the beaker. Include in your answer:
- what this tells you about the changing pH of this solution
- what this tells you about the change in amounts of H+ and OH- ions

Originally there was just base in the beaker so the colour would be (blue-purple) ph of either 8-14M But as there is acid being added the solution will begin to neutralize (ph 7) turning green M colour. If hydrochloric acid (14/M) added and over powers the OH ions of the base m the solution will turn (orange red) (ph 0-6) Base contain OH⁻ ions acid contain H⁺ ions so if there is and even amount of H⁺ and OH⁻ ions the solution is neutral es the two ions balance ec the out M

Student (b)

Year 10 Acids and Bases – Practice Question

E7
(last E point
missing)

Question 1

A student has three unlabelled beakers each containing a colourless liquid. One contains water, one contains a solution of sodium carbonate, and one contains Hydrochloric acid. To work out which liquid is which, the student put a drop from each beaker onto a piece of blue litmus paper and a piece of red litmus paper. She then added universal indicator to each beaker.

	Colour of blue litmus	Colour of red litmus	Colour of universal indicator	Name of the liquid
Beaker 1	Stays blue	Stays red	Turns green	water (neutral)
Beaker 2	Turns red	Stays red	Turns red	(acid) Hydrochloric acid
Beaker 3	Stays blue	Turns blue	Turns blue	(base) sodium carbonate A

Question 2

A beaker contains sodium hydroxide solution and 5 drops of universal indicator. hydrochloric acid was added to the beaker until no more changes were observed.

(a) Write a word equation for the reaction between hydrochloric acid and sodium hydroxide.

hydrochloric acid + sodium hydroxide
Sodium hydrochloride + water

(b) Describe how the indicator colour changes as the hydrochloric acid is added to the beaker.
Include in your answer:
- what this tells you about the changing pH of this solution
- what this tells you about the change in amounts of H+ and OH- ions

Sodium hydroxide is a base^A so if we add a UI to it,
the OH⁻ ions are → it will go purple^A. this shows the pH value is very high (10-14)
and as it's a base, it contains OH⁻ ions. if we keep adding
greater than H⁺ ions. hydrochloric acid to it, it will turn green^M which means it's
now neutral. the pH value is now 7✓. The H⁺ ions (acid)
and OH⁻ ions (base) are balanced!^A ^E If we keep adding
hydrochloric acid the H⁺ ions will be greater than the OH⁻ ^M ions
it will now turn red/orange as it becomes an acid.
The pH value is now lower than 7. Sodium hydrochlorate and
water are produced.

49

The inquiry outcomes

Data were analysed from a random sample of **grades** for the practice question on neutralisation, compared with the end-of-topic test marks. Analysis showed an effect size of 0.22 after just one lesson (Table 4.8).

Table 4.8: Effect sizes for grades of Year 10 students studying chemical reactions

	Average grade	Standard deviation
Before SOLO lesson (end-of-topic test)	4/8	1.56
After SOLO lesson	4.33/8	1.49

The following is a representative selection of **student responses** to subsequent survey questions:

- What do you think about the learning you did in the SOLO lesson?

    It was very helpful, I could also know what I need to study more or what area I am weaker in.

    I found the SOLO lesson really helpful and I learnt quite a lot.

- What SOLO activity did you find the most useful for your learning?

    Mapping concepts under multistructural and relational on large sheets of paper, using all of the information to write paragraphs about neutralisation.

    Using all of the information to write paragraphs about neutralisation.

- Did you find the new version of the learning outcomes I gave you helpful to measure your progress when you are learning?

    Yes, it was so helpful, I looked at them before the exam and found I knew them, it was like a checklist.

- Did the activity we did in class help you to know how you plan your writing?

    Yes because I linked all the information before I wrote.

Conclusion

The one lesson conducted with this science class using SOLO-based thinking had a positive effect on student learning. The test was administered without any prior warning so students were unable to revise in their own time beforehand.

There is evidence that students were using SOLO Taxonomy to help them frame their answers. However, in the cases where Merit or Excellence was not achieved, it is clear that many students did not read the question carefully. As a result, these answers, while scientifically correct, did not answer the specific question. Many students did not take notice of the bullet points provided in the question.

Case study: Using randomised controlled trials with a Year 12 science class

This inquiry examined whether a SOLO learning log with clearly defined success criteria would have a measured impact on student learning in a Year 12 chemistry class.

The sample

Two Year 12 chemistry classes were involved in this inquiry. Both classes were taught the same content (periodic trends, first ionisation energy, atomic radius, ionic radius) and completed the same activities during the four lessons. However, they differed in terms of the learning intentions they were assigned:

- The non-SOLO class worked with the learning intention and outcomes as set out in Table 4.9.
- The SOLO class worked with a SOLO-based self-assessment rubric, which set out the learning intentions and success criteria (Table 4.10).

Table 4.9: Original learning intention and outcomes for the non-SOLO Year 12 chemistry class on periodicity

Learning intention: Vertical and horizontal trends in the periodic table exist for atomic radius, ionic radius and ionisation energy.		
Learning outcomes	**Notes page(s)**	**Flip classroom**
Vertical and horizontal trends in the periodic table exist for atomic radius and ionic radius across a period.	11–13	Video Review: Trends in Atomic Radii
Vertical and horizontal trends in the periodic table exist for ionisation energy across a period.	14	Video Review: Trends in Ionisation Energies
Vertical and horizontal trends in the periodic table exist for electron affinity and electronegativity across a period.	15–17	Video Review: Trends in Electronegativity

Table 4.10: SOLO self-assessment rubric for the SOLO-based Year 12 chemistry class on periodicity

Multistructural	Relational	Extended abstract
Learning intention: Vertical and horizontal trends in the periodic table exist for atomic radius, ionic radius, melting point, and ionisation energy.		
Atomic radius decreases across a period. Atomic radius is the distance between the nucleus of two adjacent atoms.	Atomic radius decreases across a period because the number of protons in the nucleus is increasing but the number of e shells occupied remains the same.	Increased positive charge in the nucleus and similar distance from the nucleus to the valence electrons result in greater electrostatic attraction between the nucleus and the valence electrons so the radius decreases.
Ionic radius increases across a period. Ionic radius is the distance between the nucleus of two adjacent atoms.	Ionic radius is dependent on charge of the ion and number of protons in the nucleus.	Cations have formed when atoms lose electrons – more protons in the nucleus will lead to a greater electrostatic attraction between nucleus and valence electrons so the radius will decrease. Anions have formed when atoms gain electrons – more protons in the nucleus will lead to a greater electrostatic attraction between nucleus and valence electrons. However, extra electrons in the valence shell lead to greater electron repulsion so the radius will increase.
First ionisation energy is the energy needed to remove the least tightly held electron from a mole of gaseous atoms. Periodicity is the repeating pattern of properties in the periodic table.	First ionisation energy increases across a period because the number of protons in the nucleus is increasing and the number of e shells occupied remains the same. $M(g) \rightarrow M^+(g) + e^-$ Periodicity is the repeating pattern of chemical and physical properties in the periodic table.	Increased positive charge in the nucleus and similar distance from the nucleus to the valence electrons result in greater electrostatic attraction between the nucleus and the valence electrons so the first ionisation energy increases.

The task

The classes were given the same test on two separate occasions, with 10 minutes to complete each one:

- A pre-test was given without prior warning as a true measure of prior knowledge.
- A post-test was given after the teaching of the learning intentions. Students had no prior warning other than that, before the test was given out again, they were allowed five minutes to discuss their learning in groups with the learning intentions as a support for their discussions. They were not allowed to use any notes during this discussion.

The inquiry outcomes

Analysis of the **pre- and post-test results** showed that both groups experienced an effect size of greater than 0.4 (ie, above the "hinge point" or average effect). However, the effect size for the SOLO group was greater (1.35) than it was for the group that worked with the old version of the learning outcomes (0.64) (Table 4.11).

In the interests of keeping the inquiry fair, both classes were given the same notes and completed the same tasks in class. The only difference was the structure of the learning intentions and the information that students had access to with the learning intentions.

Student feedback on the SOLO-based learning intentions was also strongly positive. For example, 93 per cent found these learning intentions useful or very useful and 90 per cent considered the new version gave them greater visibility of what success looks like, compared with the old learning intentions.

Table 4.11: Effect sizes of teaching with SOLO-based version of learning outcomes versus non-SOLO version

Class	Average difference between pre- and post-test scores	Standard deviation	Effect size
SOLO-based learning outcomes	34.13	14.99	1.35
Traditional (non-SOLO) learning outcomes	20.5	20.27	0.64

Conclusions

Teaching as inquiry is an effective pedagogy to accompany evidence-based teaching. Although it is currently promoted as a new approach, teachers have always observed what happens in their classrooms and sought ways to improve student learning. They collect information from research they have read, claims they have heard at conferences and staffroom anecdotes on pedagogical approaches that work, as well as their own qualitative data. Then they refine these approaches in their own context and share student outcomes with others.

Teaching as inquiry starts with the simplest of classroom observations: qualitative data describing what happens and how we feel. For example, a teacher might observe that "sharing SOLO-coded learning intentions leads to more learning-focused students". That observation itself might seem satisfactory for a while. However, at some time, or with a particular class or an individual, it will not be enough, prompting further questions such as:

- How and why was sharing SOLO-coded learning intentions different from our previous experiences of sharing learning intentions?
- Is there a particular age, ability or student background for which sharing learning intentions works better than in other circumstances?
- Does sharing learning intentions with students work better when students co-construct the learning intentions?
- Are there other approaches to sharing learning intentions that work equally well?
- What happens to students' learning focus if we do not share learning intentions at all?
- Are other measures of students' learning focus available that might give us better data?

As the questions deepen, so the nature of the data collected changes to include quantitative and qualitative measures.

As noted in Section 1, it can be difficult for classroom practitioners to "know their effect". Teachers are often uncertain about how to reliably determine the effect of what they do. They quite rightly worry about the method they should use in teacher inquiry, what counts as an outcome, and the potential for bias. They ask if it is possible to know your effect without randomised controlled trials and meta-analyses. They do not want their pedagogical practice to rely on anecdote, opinion or ideology but they often lack the confidence and competence to undertake meaningful inquiry into the practices they adopt.

In this book, we have shared many different practical qualitative and quantitative research strategies that classroom teachers can use to monitor and evaluate the effect of using SOLO on student outcomes. The approaches are user friendly, very accessible to classroom practitioners looking for ways to reliably and validly monitor the impact of their teaching on student learning.

The case studies from teachers at St Kentigern College (New Zealand) and Clifton Community School (United Kingdom) illustrate what others have done in the context of the classroom-based use of SOLO Taxonomy. The research strategies they used can be easily adapted to any teaching context.

Effective teachers who have picked up Hattie's call to "know thy impact" will continually adapt and tweak interventions in response to their student learning outcomes. This book gives teachers many different ideas on how to do this. We conclude with a quote from Sir Michael Barber's "Joy and Data" lecture that captures our sense of the teacher as an activator. We hope this book may in some small way encourage teachers to see the "joy" in data.

> *The teacher is no longer just a transmitter of knowledge, though she or he may do this periodically, but nor is she or he a mere facilitator either. Rather the role is that of activator, in John Hattie's evocative phrase; someone who injects ambition, provokes thought, asks great questions, challenges mediocrity and brings passion and insight to the task at hand; and who at the same time, drawing on excellent data, has a clear personalized picture of every student in the class. As a result the teacher is in a position to have an informed conversation with each student about where they are, where they want to go and how they might get there.*
> (Sir Michael Barber 2015)

References

Barber, M. (2015). Joy and Data. The Australian Learning Lecture, 21 May, Melbourne. URL: www.all-learning.org.au/lecture/events/inaugural-lecture

Biggs, J and Collis, K. (1982). *Evaluating the Quality of Learning: The SOLO Taxonomy.* New York: Academic Press.

Biggs, J and Tang, C. (2007). *Teaching for Quality Learning at University: What the student does* (3rd ed). Berkshire: Society for Research into Higher Education & Open University Press.

Boulton-Lewis, GM, Smith, D, McCrindle, A, Burnett, P and Campbell, K. (2001). Secondary teachers' conceptions of teaching and learning. *Learning and Instruction* 11(1): 35–51.

Braun, V and Clarke, V. (2013). *Successful Qualitative Research: A practical guide for beginners.* London: Sage.

Burrows, R. (2013). So why SOLO for St Andrew's College? URL: https://youtu.be/zuwcRFmHQBw

Creswell, JW. (2013). *Qualitative Inquiry and Research Design: Choosing among five approaches* (3rd ed). London: Sage.

Evans, D. (2007). *Taking Sides: Clashing views on controversial issues in teaching and educational practice* (3rd ed). McGraw-Hill.

Flick, U. (2014). *An Introduction to Qualitative Research* (5th ed). London: Sage.

Goldacre, B. (2013a). *Building Evidence into Education.* London: Department of Education. URL: www.gov.uk/government/news/building-evidence-into-education

Goldacre, B. (2013b). Keynote presentation at ResearchED 2013. URL: www.researched2013.co.uk/ben-goldacres-keynote-at-researched-2013

Hattie, JAC. (2009). *Visible Learning: A synthesis of over 800 meta-analyses relating to achievement.* London: Routledge.

Hattie, JAC. (2012). *Visible Learning for Teachers: Maximising impact on learning.* London: Routledge.

Hattie, JAC and Yates, G. (2014). *Visible Learning and the Science of How We Learn.* London: Routledge.

Hook, P. (2015). *First Steps with SOLO Taxonomy: Applying the model in your classroom.* Invercargill: Essential Resources Educational Publishers Limited.

Makel, MC and Plucker, JA. (2014). Facts are more important than novelty: replication in the education sciences. *Educational Researcher* XX(10): 1–13. URL: www.aera.net/Newsroom/RecentAERAResearch/FactsAreMoreImportantThanNoveltyReplicationintheEducationSciences/tabid/15613/Default.aspx

Marzano, RJ, Pickering, D and Pollock, JE. (2001). *Classroom Instruction that Works: Research-based strategies for increasing student achievement.* Aurora, CO: Mid-Continent Research for Education and Learning.

Ministry of Education. (2007). *The New Zealand Curriculum: The English-medium teaching and learning in years 1–13.* Wellington: Learning Media.

Saljo, R. (1981). Learning approach and outcome: some empirical observations. *Instructional Science* 10(1): 47–65.

Watkins, D. (1983). Depth of processing and the quality of learning outcomes. *Instructional Science* 12: 49–58.

Wiliam, D. (2015) The research delusion. *Times Educational Supplement* April.

Zimmerman, BJ and Martinez Pons, M. (1986). Development of a structured interview for assessing student use of self-regulated learning strategies. *American Educational Research Journal* 23(4): 614–628.

Index of figures, tables and templates

Figures

Tables

Templates

Acknowledgements

Thanks to Professor John Biggs for his encouragement and ongoing critique of our work with the classroom-based approach to using SOLO Taxonomy and to the many teachers and schools in New Zealand, Australia and the United Kingdom who are conducting teacher inquiries into the classroom-based use of SOLO Taxonomy. Special thanks to staff and students at St Kentigern College (Auckland, New Zealand) for the many case studies used in the book; Pat Baird, Ross Gerritson, Gerard Hodgson, Emily Coleborne, Jess Acheson and Chay Carter. Our thanks to the St Kentigern Board of Trustees, which generously approved study leave for a term so that Tabitha Leonard could conduct research for the examples used in the text. Thanks also to Clifton Community School (Rotherham, South Yorkshire, United Kingdom) for data used in the science case study in Section 4.